Managing *the* Classroom

Creating a Culture for Primary and Elementary Teaching and Learning

Third Edition

Billie J. Enz
Sharon A. Kortman
Arizona State University

Connie J. Honaker
Boise State University

KENDALL/HUNT PUBLISHING COMPANY
4050 Westmark Drive   Dubuque, Iowa 52002

Book Team

Chairman and Chief Executive Officer   Mark C. Falb
President and Chief Operating Officer   Chad M. Chandlee
Vice President, Higher Education   David L. Tart
Director of National Book Program   Paul B. Carty
Editorial Development Manager   Georgia Botsford
Developmental Editor   Denise LaBudda
Assistant Vice President, Production Services   Christine E. O'Brien
Senior Production Editor   Carrie Maro
Permissions Editor   Renae Horstman
Cover Designer   Janell Edwards

Cover image © bonniej © 2008, istockphoto

BRIEF CONTENTS

CONTENTS

All students deserve a quality educator. In education there is the combination of the art and science of the profession that allows an individual to be successful and to fulfill expectations of that quality. The science of teaching includes content and professional knowledge: knowledge of pedagogy, human development, and teaching standards. More specifically, it includes lesson planning and implementation, management design, assessment tools, and communication plans. The art of teaching is creating that special environment in the classroom that allows the curriculum to come alive for the students. It provides the connection to relationships and motivation for learning. It bridges the planning of good teaching to effective implementation of that teaching.

Managing the Classroom: Creating a Culture for Primary and Elementary Teaching and Learning is a book that provides teachers with the resources of bringing together the art and science into the reality of teaching practice. It addresses the day-to-day details that help make a classroom environment conducive to student learning. It is obvious that the research on effective teaching is embedded within the practical applications provided to help a teacher from the beginning to end of a school year, and throughout their professional career.

As leaders in a suburban school district in the Phoenix metropolitan area, we have an expectation for excellence in everything we do. Since implementing the BEST (Beginning Educator Support Team) induction and mentoring program in the Apache Junction Unified School District, we provide teachers with this resource. The support provides a positive start and ongoing assistance to our teachers, as evidenced by quality teaching performance.

Gregory A. Wyman, Ed.D.

Superintendent, Apache Junction Unified School District

The first day, week, month, and year of school are simultaneously exciting and overwhelming; rewarding and frustrating; energizing and exhausting. These are all normal responses to the expectations placed on educators. *Managing the Classroom: Creating a Culture for Primary and Elementary Teaching and Learning* is designed to provide explicit information about the demands, decisions, and details teachers deal with on a daily basis. The content of the text focuses on helping teachers ground themselves in professional teaching standards while they evolve their practice.

Managing the Classroom: Creating a Culture for Primary and Elementary Teaching and Learning is organized into six chapters that parallel the responsibilities of teachers as they progress through the school year. Each chapter includes two comprehensive divisions that provide in-depth information, detailed examples, case studies, and vignettes to help educators develop a thorough understanding of concepts related to managing the classroom.

1. **What Is Management of Teaching?**—helps the education professional become familiar with the diverse role of teaching. This section helps the teacher learn skills and techniques that foster relationships with school colleagues, parents, and agencies in the larger community to support students' learning and well-being. It also outlines school-wide policies and procedures.

2. **Management: Managing the Classroom Culture**—features information for proactively organizing the classroom, which contributes significantly to a well-managed classroom. Next, the text offers information about the continuum of behavior management approaches. This section also helps teachers better understand and articulate their own management philosophy and create a learning environment that encourages positive social interaction, active engagement in learning, and self-motivation.

3. **Instructional Design and Instruction: Managing Student Learning**—discusses how the teacher's planning contributes to effective learning and positive student behavior, and reviews a range of instructional strategies that contribute to student retention. This section also offers explicit guidance to help teachers work with students with diverse learning and language needs.

4. **Assessment: Managing Student Progress**—offers explicit information that helps the teacher understand and use formal and informal assessment strategies, to evaluate and ensure the continuous intellectual and social development of their learners.

5. **Collaboration: Managing Communications**—reviews strategies for proactive, positive interactions with parents and families. Further, this section discusses approaches to communicating with members of the school community, such as building supportive relationships with mentors and administrators.

6. **Professional Development: Managing Reflective Growth**—highlights techniques that help the teaching professional maintain self-management, personally and professionally. Finally the chapter discusses dozens of suggestions that help students continue to learn until the last minute of the school year. It also provides opportunities for the teacher to reflect and plan for more professional and personal growth.

SPECIAL FEATURES

In the text you will see accented material which contains the following:

best PRACTICES

In addition to researched best practices embedded within chapter content, these Best Practice highlights provide a specific research report aligned to chapter curriculum.

ASSESSMENTS

Assessments are built into the text for introductory points of inquiry, discussion, and review, and self-assessments of professional growth. Look for them in context to guide your reflections. Next steps are included to record your professional goals for future action.

 This disc symbol means that the page is located on the CD-ROM and is available for your immediate use.

view POINT

- Information that deals with district/school policy, procedures, and/or school etiquette.

- Items that are words to the wise and may save you time, energy and/or effort.

- Suggestions to enhance planning and teaching time.

Mentor Voices

➤ Mentors provide tips and time-savers related to chapter content.

ACKNOWLEDGMENTS

The authors wish to acknowledge teachers who are committed to positively impacting students. We applaud you for your dedication to continuous growth and development.

We acknowledge the contributions of Barbara Carlile, Veronica J. Lyons, Kathleeen Rutowski, and Gloria Smith.

We acknowledge our families for their support. We applaud your active engagement in our lives.

We acknowledge each other as valued colleagues working together to uphold our profession. We applaud each other's areas of strength and expertise, and the collaborations that weave our efforts together.

A SPECIAL THANK YOU

Kudos times ten to Joanna Honea for her quality technical assistance and dedicated work. We appreciate your contributions.

A special thanks to Katie Riffle and Katrina Cervantes for your behind-the-scenes research and work.

REVIEWERS

We gratefully acknowledge the constructive comments of the colleagues who provided reviews of this text:

Anita Absher, University of Texas Permian Basin

Ann Adkins, Dana College

Derek Anderson, Northern Michigan University

Kathleen Bernhard, Hudson Valley Community College

Jeff Blacklock, Midwestern State University

Barbara Brock, Creighton University

Susan Cagley, Baptist Bible College

Elizabeth Cashing, St. Bonaventure University

Richard Castelluccio, University of Cincinnati

Francie Christopher, Northwest Missouri State University

Glen Clark, Utah Valley State College

Christy Cornelius, Jefferson College

Michele Dickey-Kotz, Graceland University

Kathy Doody, SUNY Buffalo State College

Tom Drummond, North Seattle Community College

Karen Eifler, University of Portland

Claude Endfield, Northland Pioneer College E

Lynne Ensworth, University of Northern Iowa

Max Fridell, Northwest Missouri State University

Ron Fritsch, Texas Woman's University

Robert Gates, Bloomsburg University

Mary Ann Gray-Schlegel, Millersville University of PA

Mary Harris, College of the Southwest

Ray Heitzmann, Villanova University

Dr. Gwyn Herman, University of Mary

Belinda Hill, Saint Martin's University

Sara Horton, Stonehill College

Antoinette Howard, Hudson Valley Community College

Frank Howe, Longwood University

Harold Hoyle, Santa Clara University

Michael Kallam, Southeastern Oklahoma State University

Frank Kawtoski, Eastern University

Debra Knaebel, Indiana State University

Debora Kuchey, Xavier University

Dannielle Leaverton, St. Martin's University

Kerbe Lee, Martin Methodist College

David Little, Samford University

Kimberly Loomis, Kennesaw State University

Michelle Lundgren, Grace University

Margaret Malenka, Michigan State University

Roberta Martel, Leeward Community College

David Meckley, University of Nevada, Las Vegas

Joann Migyanka, Indiana University of Penn

Debra Mills, Missouri Valley College

Courtney Moffatt, Edgewood College

Dawn Munson, Elgin Community College

Cecilia Pierce, UAB School of Education

Veronica Plumb, University of Alaska–Fairbanks

BethAnne Pruitt, Eastern Kentucky University

Susan Rakow, Cleveland State University

Kathryn Roe, William Penn College

Marjorie Schiller, Central Ariz College–Coolidge

Donna Scoggins, University of Arkansas–Fort Smith

Bradley Sidle, Wright State University

Audrey Skrupskelis, University of South Carolina–Aiken

Judy Terpstra, Southern Connecticut State University

Patrick Thomas, Armstrong Atlantic State University

Joseph Austin Vasek, University of Mary Hardin–Baylor

Helen Wall, Troy State University–Dothan

Susan Woron, Delaware County Community College

Billie J. Enz (Ph.D. Elementary Education) is the Associate Dean of the School of Educational Innovation and Teacher Preparation at Arizona State University's Polytechnic Campus. Dr. Enz has authored several books on new teacher development and mentor training, including: *The Student Teaching Experience: A Developmental Approach, Coaching the Student Teacher: A Developmental Approach, Blue Print for Teaching and Life Cycle of the Career Teacher*. Dr. Enz is a member of the Early Childhood faculty, and teaches language and literacy courses. She has numerous articles and texts in this area, including *Teaching Language and Literacy: From Preschool to the Elementary Grades and Helping Young Children Learn Language and Literacy: From Birth through Preschool*.

Sharon A. Kortman (Ed.D. Curriculum and Instruction) is Director of Beginning Educator Support Team (BEST) in the College of Education, Arizona State University, and an inductee in ASU's Hall of Fame. Dr. Kortman's research and consulting emphases are directly related to her leadership in university/district partnerships, locally and nationally, providing comprehensive support, training, and resources in teacher induction, mentoring and coaching, teaching standards, and shared administrative leadership. Dr. Kortman is co-author of *The BEST Beginning Teacher Experience: A Framework for Professional Development, The BEST Mentoring Experience: A Framework for Professional Development, The BEST Standards in Teaching*, and a series of other publications supporting teachers and teacher-leaders through their professional growth.

Connie J. Honaker (M.Ed English and Educational Leadership) has taught at all levels. She has also served in various administrative roles. Connie takes special pride in being the founding principal of a large comprehensive high school. She is the recipient of the Arizona Distinguished Administrator of the Year Award from the Arizona School Administrators Association. She has collaborated to establish partnerships with school districts to bring induction and mentoring to educators within their districts. These roles have given her insight into the needs of teachers and administrators. This has prepared her for her authorships and current work as instructor and field experiences coordinator at Boise State University.

What Is Management of Teaching?

1

> **❝** To teach is to transform by informing, to develop a zest for lifelong learning, to help pupils become students—mature independent learners, architects of an exciting, challenging future. Teaching at its best is a kind of communion, a meeting and merging of minds. **❞**
>
> —EDGAR DALE

Have you ever put together a thousand-piece jigsaw puzzle without a sample of the completed picture? That is how a teacher described his efforts to organize and manage his classroom. The purpose of this book is to provide essential information to help educators prepare for and successfully negotiate their school year.

Knowing how to prepare yourself and your classroom prior to the start of the school year may predict your success as a teacher. Chapter 1 offers information that will assist you in your professional understanding of the teaching standards, and in the organization of your teaching role.

POINTS OF INQUIRY

- How will you exhibit professionalism in relationship to your school system and in interactions with colleagues, parents and students?
- How will you use the teaching standards to frame your practice?
- What is your plan for promoting positive relationships in your teaching community?
- What systems of organization will assist in fulfilling your teaching role?

The Diverse Role of Teaching

> **"**Good teaching comes from the identity and integrity of the teacher. Good teachers join self and subject and students in the fabric of life.**"**
>
> – PARKER J. PALMER

Professionalism

Successful educators are professional in their attitudes, behaviors, and skills. They thoughtfully respond to established policies, and consistently implement appropriate classroom procedures. Professionalism also pertains to how the teacher interacts with students, parents, and the school system. The following offers several aspects of professionalism.

PROFESSIONALISM WITH STUDENTS

- Maintains accurate records (attendance and grades) according to school procedure.
- Reviews policies and procedures with students at the beginning of the year and throughout the year as needed.
- Holds all students accountable for following school rules, policies, and procedures, such as attendance, homework, and classroom behavior.

PROFESSIONALISM WITH PARENTS

- Informs parents of policies and procedures, and confirms they have received the information.
- Communicates information to parents about student progress, attendance, and classroom behavior.
- Documents conversations with parents regarding student progress.

PROFESSIONALISM WITHIN THE SCHOOL

- Maintains confidentiality regarding student records and school personnel.
- Participates in professional growth opportunities.
- Models appropriate behavior, demeanor, language, dress, and humor.
- Maintains strong work ethic, including:
  - punctuality and adherence to professional workday;
  - attending department and faculty meetings;
  - completing paperwork in a timely manner;
  - being prepared to teach and promptly grade assignments;
  - cooperating with faculty, staff and administration.

Teaching Standards in Practice

Teaching standards are similar in all educational settings, outlining the expectations of you in your teaching role. Your understanding of the teaching standards will determine the learning in your classroom, and will link the teaching standards to student standards.

COMMON VOCABULARY

Standards provide educators with a common vocabulary. When teaching standards are defined, educators understand expectations of performance. Teachers can identify their strengths and focus on areas of need when developing and implementing yearly professional goals.

Examples of teaching standards include:

- Content Knowledge
- Professional Knowledge
- Instructional Design
- Instruction
- Management
- Assessment
- Collaboration
- Professional Development

view POINT

Decisions about your commitment to the profession are made quickly. Remember to sign up for a faculty committee, sponsor a school activity and/or share ideas graciously.

COLLABORATION

Standards create an organized method to collaborate on effective practices. By department or by school, educators can document their work for specific best practices aligned with each standard.

COMMUNICATION

Standards implementation needs to be communicated. If educators have the same mission, think of the impact to student achievement. Priority time needs to be given to explain purpose, develop, understand, and practice teaching to the standards. A thorough understanding of their benefits and a plan for support are essential.

Relationships

Educators can increase student learning through building positive relationships in the school community and with their students. Research shows that students who are emotionally secure in the classroom have higher learning gains than students who are anxious or stressed. Therefore, it is critical that teachers take the time to analyze the effect of their behaviors and the systems they employ to encourage their students to feel a sense of belonging, be willing to take risks in their learning, and take pride in their work.

☑ **Review the following checkpoints to help you develop positive working relationships.**

- ❑ Establish contact—*relate to the individual*
- ❑ High expectations—*reasonable and revealed*
- ❑ Know students—*connect with personal interests and abilities*
- ❑ Be yourself—*share your personal interests and abilities*
- ❑ Active listening—*attentive with eye contact*
- ❑ Empathetic—*non-judgmental, from their viewpoint*
- ❑ Involvement—*supporting extra-curricular activities*
- ❑ Courteous—*exhibiting simple kindnesses*
- ❑ Fair—*not sameness, but fairness*
- ❑ Respectful of differences—*without criticism*
- ❑ Care—*check student perspectives*
- ❑ Understanding—*yet hold standards high*
- ❑ Passion for learning—*enjoy the moment*
- ❑ Love of kids—*see the joy, live vicariously*
- ❑ Humor—*laugh together*
- ❑ Belonging—*everyone has a place*
- ❑ Engagement—*being fully present*
- ❑ Motivating—*find the good*

best PRACTICES

Three primary indicators of professionalism as identified by Phelps (2006) are responsibility, respect, and risk-taking. These terms are defined as:

- Responsibility—teachers fully accept the challenges of teaching;
- Respect—teachers use respect as a touchstone for their actions;
- Risk-taking—teachers who take risks for the sake of better student learning will make greater impact on students.

When teachers are committed to these values,
their behaviors will reveal greater professionalism.

Phelps, P.H. (2006, Winter). The three Rs of professionalism. *Kappa Delta Pi Record, 42*(2), 69–71.

Questions for Reflection

evaluation
QUESTIONS?

- How will you exhibit professionalism in relationship to your school system and in interactions with colleagues, parents, and students?

- How will you use the teaching standards to frame your practice?

PROFESSIONALISM

- How will you build your professional relationship with students?
- How will you establish and maintain your professional relationship with parents?
- How will you develop your professional relationships within your school community?

TEACHING STANDARDS IN PRACTICE

- How will you gain understanding of the teaching standards identified within your state and district?
- How will you determine your strengths and needed areas of growth related to the teaching standards to outline professional goals?
- How will you align the teaching standards to student content standards?

Readiness

"Do not be tense, just be ready, not thinking but not dreaming, not being set but being flexible. It is being 'wholly' and quietly alive, aware and alert, ready for whatever may come."

—BRUCE LEE

Knowing the Community

Becoming acquainted with your community is essential to your success as a teacher. It is important for you to feel comfortable in your environment. If you are new to your community, you may have many questions about the area. Some common concerns to consider include:

COMMUTING

Learn your schedule and the flow of "commuting" traffic. Drive a few trial runs to school during the times when you would normally commute. For example, if you plan to drive to school each morning, drive it at least once during the time you would normally commute to school to find the best route, and to check traffic patterns and time. The same can be said if you plan to use subways, trains and buses.

NEWS

Subscribe to a local newspaper. Suburban and local newspapers generally carry more school and local news than large city newspapers and help the teacher become attuned to local attitudes, concerns, ideas and values.

☑️ Other areas to check for new-to-the-community teachers may include:

- ❑ Housing
- ❑ Emergency phone numbers
- ❑ Medical facilities
- ❑ Child care
- ❑ Grocery store, pharmacy, bookstores, shopping malls
- ❑ Post office location and zip code
- ❑ Utility companies that serve your area
- ❑ Recreation, exercise, sports activities and parks
- ❑ Public library
- ❑ College or university
- ❑ Radio and television stations
- ❑ Banking institutions
- ❑ Religious institutions

■■ © 2008 Jupiter Images Corporation.

District and School Contacts

Almost all healthy adults have a basic need to belong and gain acceptance in their work environment. To be successful as a teacher, you will need to orient yourself to the physical environment, learn who does what and figure out how to accomplish your instructional goals. You will also need to develop positive professional relationships with administrators, staff and colleagues, and become part of the school community.

However, becoming a part of the school community is not always an easy task. Teachers are inundated with dozens of new names and faces. There never seems to be enough time to learn all the new information and manage all the new responsibilities. The following list provides simple hints to help you fit in with your colleagues and adjust to your work environment.

- Eat lunch with other teachers as often as possible. In addition to socializing, it is important to take at least 15–20 minutes to eat, rest a moment, and share ideas and concerns.

- Make financial contributions to school collections for wedding or baby shower gifts, hospital flowers, birthday cakes and cards. This monetary token indicates your willingness to become part of a caring, collegial community.

- Smile, make positive comments to others, share ideas when asked, and graciously accept ideas when they are offered. These actions allow your colleagues to know that you are open to suggestions, advice and friendship.

- Discover who has expertise in specialized areas, such as technology, art and musical talents, and classroom management. Collaborate to share skills and talents.

- Be polite to everyone, but avoid frequent contact with colleagues who initiate negative attitudes, conversations, and behavior. Sustaining a positive attitude is key to building collegial relationships.

Learning who's who and what they do is critical. In addition to remembering names and faces of district/school staff, you should be aware of job descriptions. The following section provides a sample of job titles with spaces for names, phone numbers and e-mail addresses. A brief job description is also included. You will also want the contact information for both the district and the school office. This information may be included in your personalized planning system.

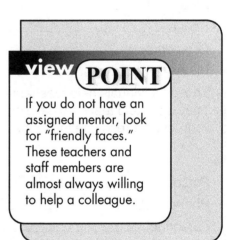

view POINT

If you do not have an assigned mentor, look for "friendly faces." These teachers and staff members are almost always willing to help a colleague.

DISTRICT INFORMATION

Phone _____ Fax _____ E-mail _____

Address _____

District Office Personnel

Superintendent _____

Phone _____ E-mail _____

This person is the educational leader of the district and is legally responsible for all district personnel and district policies and procedures.

Personnel Director _____

Phone _____ E-mail _____

This person is responsible for conducting job searches, interviews, and hiring. This person also manages payroll, deductions, and usually helps you enroll for health insurance.

Substitute Clerk _____

Phone _____ E-mail _____

This is the person you call when you need a substitute.

Transportation Director _____

Phone _____ E-mail _____

This person schedules buses for field trip transportation, in addition to managing the district's transportation systems daily.

Staff Development Office and Resource Center

Personnel _____

Phone _____ E-mail _____

Personnel _____

Phone _____ E-mail _____

These individuals help teachers expand instructional skills and develop professionally. They also help teachers develop curriculum and can help locate and select appropriate instructional resource materials.

Other

Personnel _____

Phone _____ E-mail _____

Personnel _____

Phone _____ E-mail _____

Personnel _____

Phone _____ E-mail _____

SCHOOL BUILDING INFORMATION

Phone _____ Fax _____ E-mail _____

Address _____

School Building Personnel

Principal _____

Phone _____ E-mail _____

This administrator is the educational leader of the school. It is the principal who sets the philosophical direction and work climate of the school site. The principal conducts evaluations of your teaching performance.

Assistant Principal _____

Phone _____ E-mail _____

This person deals directly with student discipline and attendance. Typically the size of the school population determines the number of assistant principals.

Secretary/s _____

Phone _____ E-mail _____

These staff members are responsible for establishing and maintaining school routines. Secretaries know where things are located and are usually willing to help teachers understand procedures for attendance, field trips and the like.

Clerk/s _____

Phone _____ E-mail _____

This person supports the secretary in the day-to-day management of the school office. This person can usually show you how to run the copy machine, fax machine, manage district software, etc.

Nurse/s _____

Phone _____ E-mail _____

These staff members are responsible for managing the health care records of the students and conduct hearing and vision tests. The nurse maintains immunization records and calls parents if a student is ill.

Building Manager/s _____

Phone _____ E-mail _____

These employees are responsible for the maintenance of the school site – doing repairs, adjusting desks, and locating classroom furniture.

Counselor/s _____

Phone _____ E-mail _____

These faculty members manage the student academic schedules and provide support to students and parents in making educational decisions.

Mentor _____

Phone _____ E-mail _____

A mentor will answer day-to-day questions, help you plan and reflect on instructional and management practices, and provide support to anything else related to your role as teacher.

GRADE LEVEL PERSONNEL

An effective grade level team can achieve results far greater than one individual working alone. It is important to develop a collegial relationship with your team.

Team Leader _____

Phone _____ E-mail _____

Team Member _____

Phone _____ E-mail _____

Team Member _____

Phone _____ E-mail _____

Team Member _____

Phone _____ E-mail _____

Team Member _____

Phone _____ E-mail _____

Special Resource/Assistance Staff

The titles of these individuals may vary from school to school. They may be called Special Education resource teachers or English Language Learner instructors. It is essential to learn these staff members' names, titles and specific responsibilities, as they will contribute to your success in the classroom.

Name	Role	Phone	E-mail

School-wide Policies and Procedures

The district/school employee handbook is probably the best source of information about school policies and procedures that are specific to your school. Policies are the rules or guidelines that govern the daily management of the school, while procedures are the specific steps required to accomplish certain policies. For example:

The school policy regarding attendance reads:

"The teacher is responsible for taking and reporting student attendance accurately at the beginning of each day and after each recess, lunch, and specials class. All teachers must record student absences."

The school attendance procedures include:

1. Take roll in the first 10 minutes of class and report to school office.

2. Inform students/parents of students' attendance status on report card.

3. Submit monthly information to the school office on the last day of the month.

You are held accountable for knowing and upholding the school's policies and procedures regarding students, instructions, and administrative concerns.

© Lisa F. Young 2008. Used under license from Shutterstock, Inc.

view POINT

After each break in the school day (recess, lunch, special classes), the teacher should do a head count to confirm all students who began the day are still present; if any student is missing, inform school administration immediately.

STUDENT CONCERNS

How Do I . . .

- Grade and report student progress? _____

  _____

- Secure health care for students? _____

  _____

- Access student information? _____

  _____

- Make student referrals? _____

  _____

- Assign homework? _____

  _____

- Respond to emergency situations, such as fire, tornado, earthquake, or bomb threat?

  _____

  _____

INSTRUCTIONAL NEEDS

How Do I . . .

- Check out audio-visual equipment? _____

  _____

- Collaborate with special-education staff? _____

  _____

- Collaborate with English-language learner staff? _____

  _____

- Schedule and conduct field trips? _____

  _____

- Order trade books? _____

  _____

- Order resources, materials and supplies? _____

  _____

ADMINISTRATIVE ISSUES

How Do I . . .

- Report attendance/tardies? _____

  _____

- Secure a substitute? _____

  _____

- Reinforce a school-wide discipline plan? _____

  _____

- Raise funds? _____

  _____

Faculty Handbook

The faculty handbook will contain policies and procedures that are vital to you as a staff member. You are responsible for knowing the contents. For example:

- Needed parent notification prior to students viewing videos in the classroom;
- Field trip procedure;
- Student arrival times;
- District policies regarding mandatory discipline code;
- Application process for leadership opportunities.

Don't let your faculty handbook collect dust. This is an important document you need to reference prior to seeking assistance. In addition to the information provided in the handbook, this is an appropriate place to file updates throughout the school year from the district, administration, or department.

Mentor Assignment

Many districts offer opportunities for mentorship. This reciprocal relationship can be a key to your success as an educator, and can enrich your professional growth. Check with your school system for the procedure to sign up.

District/School Discipline Code

As you design your own classroom management plan, review and align to district board mandated discipline requirements. For example, know your responsibility when an altercation may occur in your presence. Many of these mandatory policies and procedures are directly linked to the legal system, and require compliance.

In addition, there are mandatory school policies that must be enforced. For example, tardies and absences must be reported according to state law, and are a consideration of student safety. Another example is the use of profanity in the classroom. This may occur in your classroom, but the consequence may include a school policy and not be within your authority as a teacher. This will need to be reported to administration. This process allows administration to identify a student who may be having difficulty in school, and offer resources for support.

view POINT

An effective way to organize your calendar, schedules and additional information quickly is to create an A to Z section in your notebook. File the calendar under "C" and the schedule under "S." Label each inclusion in the upper right-hand corner for easy retrieval.

Calendaring

Keeping track of both immediate (daily/weekly) and long-range (monthly/yearly) deadlines is essential for effective teachers. Use a school calendar or transfer dates to your own working calendar. Many schools also publish weekly updates that are invaluable for keeping up with committee meetings and paperwork deadlines.

Organizational and Curriculum Planning

Your lesson plan book is one of the main keys to organizing and managing your time and the curriculum. Many teachers find the standard commercial lesson plan book difficult to use; it is hard to write all of your thoughts in the small boxes typically provided. One suggestion that can be helpful is to develop an individualized planning system, a teaching organizer.

This section provides models and samples of planning schemata, and suggestions that might help you organize critical information. Begin by purchasing a large three-ring binder. Copy any of the forms illustrated in this section you believe to be useful. You may modify these forms or create new forms that are appropriate for your needs. Finally, organize the sections in your planning book for flexibility in adapting to daily teaching needs.

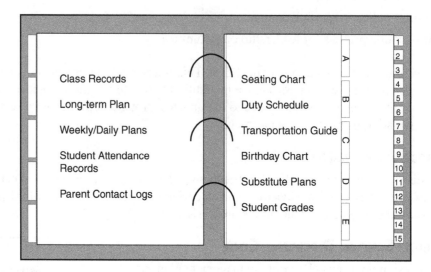

Possible Contents

Class Records These include students' names, phone numbers, addresses, and special notes about the students; for example, parents' surname (if different from the student's) and/or information about a student's physical needs. The class record may also be used to organize a student code system that helps alphabetize materials.

Long-term Plan A year-long curriculum overview helps you plan ahead for needed resources and supplemental materials, maximizes content integration, and allows you to make the most effective use of instructional time. To begin, work with your department chair, mentor teacher or grade-level team, and review the district curriculum guide for scope and sequence.

Weekly/Daily Plans A week-long outline/overview for the instructional events that will occur in the classroom includes a timeframe with "skeletal" daily plans. Be sure to consult or collaborate with Special Education teachers or personnel supporting students in your classroom.

Mentor Voices

➤ "Get to know the administrative assistants and your custodian. They are a wealth of information."

Student Attendance Records Keeping your attendance log close at hand is essential for accurately tracking attendance and communicating attendance concerns to parents and school administrators. All teachers are required to monitor student attendance.

Parent Contact Logs Teachers should document calls made to parents. The contact log should provide specific information about the time and date of the call, the name of the parent/guardian you spoke to, the reason for the call, the parental response to the positive feedback or noted area of concern, and, finally, any actions that need to be taken.

Special Features The notebook may also include:

- Seating chart/s
- Duty schedule
- Transportation guide
- Birthday chart
- Substitute plans
- Student grades

The Long-Term Planning Realities

To begin to get "the whole picture," a teacher should plan a tentative year-long topical overview. Knowing what lies ahead gives you an opportunity to see how you can make all the curricular pieces fit together smoothly. To begin this process, consult the district curriculum guide and discuss plans with your grade-level leader, mentor, or a colleague who teaches the same content.

© 2008 Jupiter Images Corporation, Inc.

> ## Mentor Voices
>
> ➤ "Keep an organized documentation system. You never know when you'll need to refer to something from a prior conversation or meeting."

LONG-TERM CURRICULUM PLANNING GUIDE

Content Area _____

Month	Curriculum Plan	Student Standards
August		
September		
October		
November		
December		
January		
February		
March		
April		
May		
June/July		

According to Kortman and Honaker (2005), application of the teaching standards provides a direct correlation to an increase in quality teaching. When teachers are conscious of their abilities in the standard areas, their awareness of strengths and needed areas of improvement are more clearly articulated. In addition, teaching standards can be applied to staff development, professional development goals, teacher evaluation, mentoring, career advancement, teacher effectiveness and student achievement.

> *" Teaching standards create a definitive criterion for equality that will provide all students with an equal advantage to excellence in education . . . Understanding and being able to specifically describe what we do is critical to our profession and the students we serve. The standards 'raise the bar'."*

Kortman, S. A., & Honaker, C. J. (2005). *The best standards in teaching: Reflection to quality practice.* Dubuque, IA: Kendall/Hunt Publishing Company.

Questions for Reflection

evaluation QUESTIONS

- What is your plan for promoting positive relationships in your teaching community?
- What systems of organization will assist in fullfilling your teaching role?

BUILDING RELATIONSHIPS

- How will you initiate positive student relationships?
- How will you cultivate student relationships?
- How will you mediate relationships for an effective working environment?

READINESS

- How will you keep track of the school calendar and school schedules?
- How will you decide your daily teaching schedule?
- How will you ensure you are following policies in the faculty handbook?
- How will you develop curriculum plans?
- How will you organize and manage student information?
- How will you track daily lessons and manage details?

Self-Assessment of Professional Growth

Name				Date	
Grade Level/Content Area					

Professionalism	Low				High
To what degree do I have the knowledge needed to exhibit professionalism in my school system?	1 ☐	2 ☐	3 ☐	4 ☐	5 ☐
To what degree do I have the skills needed to exhibit professionalism in my school system?	1 ☐	2 ☐	3 ☐	4 ☐	5 ☐
Teaching Standards in Practice	Low				High
To what degree do I have the knowledge needed to effectively use the teaching standards in my practice?	1 ☐	2 ☐	3 ☐	4 ☐	5 ☐
To what degree do I have the skills needed to effectively use the teaching standards in my practice?	1 ☐	2 ☐	3 ☐	4 ☐	5 ☐
Building Relationships	Low				High
To what degree do I have the knowledge needed to promote positive relationships in my teaching community?	1 ☐	2 ☐	3 ☐	4 ☐	5 ☐
To what degree do I have the skills needed to promote positive relationships in my teaching community?	1 ☐	2 ☐	3 ☐	4 ☐	5 ☐
Readiness	Low				High
To what degree do I have the knowledge needed to be organized in my teaching role?	1 ☐	2 ☐	3 ☐	4 ☐	5 ☐
To what degree do I have the skills needed to be organized in my teaching role?	1 ☐	2 ☐	3 ☐	4 ☐	5 ☐

Next Steps

Design goals for setting yourself up for success as a professional educator.

_____

_____

_____

_____

_____

_____

_____

_____

_____

_____

_____

_____

_____

_____

_____

_____

_____

_____

_____

_____

_____

Management: Managing the Classroom Culture

> "Effective classroom management is the major pre-requisite to effective instruction."
>
> —WILLFORD A. WEBER

The classroom environment you create reflects your teaching style and your beliefs about teaching. Organizing the learning environment and managing student engagement are critical to developing a positive classroom culture. Even the way you organize desks and display work will make students feel welcome, encourage them to learn, and motivate positive behavior. Building this positive classroom climate requires thoughtful planning and a knowledgeable skilled teacher. The teacher must simultaneously consider a number of building blocks that must be carefully placed into a management framework. This chapter provides specific suggestions to consider as you prepare your classroom to be organized and efficient for working and learning.

POINTS OF INQUIRY

- How will you set up your classroom to accommodate organizational needs and student learning?

- What is your plan for an effective start to the school year?

- How will you reinforce learning and behavioral expectations in the classroom?

- What strategies will you implement to develop self-directed students?

Building Blocks of Management

Organization of the Learning Environment

> "Organizations are of two kinds, those which aim at getting something done, and those which aim at preventing something from being done."
>
> — BERTRAND RUSSELL

Classroom Set-up

viewPOINT

Creating a comfortable environment is important for your professional and personal well-being and sets you up to remain positive in your work setting. Consider keeping the following items in your classroom:

- High protein and carbohydrate snacks
- Radio, CD player or iPod
- Jacket
- Umbrella
- Comfortable shoes

viewPOINT

Plan an area for students to turn in work. Make sure you have enough space for an organized system.

To set up your classroom effectively, you will need a proactive plan for classroom design and a professional planning system.

CLASSROOM DESIGN

Not all classrooms are created equal. Some rooms are perfectly square, while others feel more like a wedge of pie. Some rooms are large with a high ceiling and skylights; some are small and dark. Some rooms have built-in storage cabinets, shelves and closets, while other rooms may only be endowed with four walls. The first rule of classroom design is to "work with the space you are given."

CLASSROOM CONSIDERATIONS

You can maximize the space you have by thoughtful planning. Begin by drawing a floor plan of the classroom. Be sure to identify where the doors and windows are located, and label any unique features, such as a sink, bathroom, or closet. Next, identify electrical outlets, whiteboards, bulletin boards, and/or stationary technologies.

After you have drawn your classroom floor plan, consider arrangement of furniture and equipment. Veteran teachers suggest you make several copies of the floor plan and experiment with furniture arrangement on paper before you begin to move desks and tables. You will probably experiment with a variety of classroom arrangements. However you decide to arrange students, you will need to consider:

Sight Students' attention is sustained longer when they can clearly see the teacher and any frequently used instructional areas.

- Can all students see the whiteboard or monitors easily?
- Are students with visual impairments seated appropriately?

Traffic Flow Cluttered classrooms are distracting, and can be dangerous. Make sure you plan your space to accommodate for student movement and safety.

- Are the aisles between desks and tables wide enough so that you and the students can move easily from one part of the room to another?
- Are storage areas, supply areas, and exits clear?

Accessibility Teachers who can view the whole classroom at a glance and quickly move about the classroom have greater control of student behavior and thus maximize learning.

- Can you see all students in the room?
- Are the aisles and doorways easily accessible for those who are physically challenged?

Instructional Match Your organization of students' desks usually reflects your beliefs about instruction and how students learn.

- Does the seating arrangement support your instructional practices?
- Does the seating arrangement facilitate student learning?

Flexibility An effective teacher uses a variety of instructional strategies to accommodate student learning.

- Can desks be moved easily if you need more space for a variety of activities?
- Can student chairs be moved easily to pair with small groups for discussion?

Functional Logic Teachers need to make sure learning areas are well planned. This occurs when teachers logically consider the functions of these areas and make good use of classroom space. For instance:

- Can you accommodate for learning activities that need clean-up?
- Are resource or writing areas placed appropriately for independent work?
- Is the science lab close to sunlight or bright artificial light so science projects can be easily sustained?
- Is technology located close to electrical outlets and in a place for visibility to all students?
- Are all areas accessible to students who have special needs?

WALL SPACE AND BULLETIN BOARDS

The way you utilize wall space and the types of bulletin boards you create send a powerful message about the tone of your classroom. Blank walls may transmit a cold feeling, while bright colors and interesting, purposeful displays engage your students.

Some schools have specific, framed corkboards for you to use for displays. Some schools have corkboard walls where almost all wall space can be used to exhibit content displays and student work. Teachers may feel overwhelmed when they begin to plan bulletin boards. Remember, you do not have to have every bit of wall space decorated before school starts. In fact, you will want to provide adequate wall space for your students to share their school work and artistic creations.

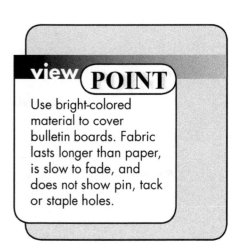

view POINT

Use bright-colored material to cover bulletin boards. Fabric lasts longer than paper, is slow to fade, and does not show pin, tack or staple holes.

Design functional bulletin boards that share specific information, remind students about classroom expectations, and motivate student learning. From the following checklist, identify the bulletin board and wall space ideas most appropriate for your grade level or content area. For the following examples, feel free to adapt to your classroom setting.

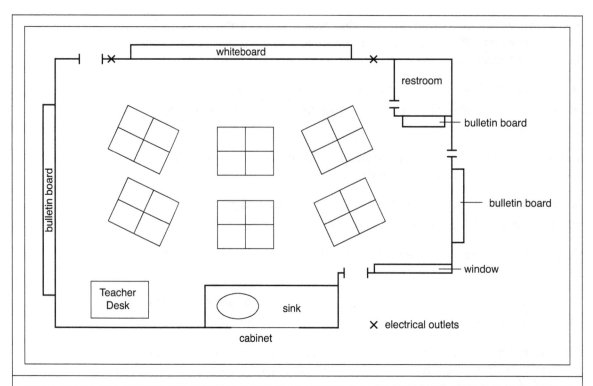

whiteboard

restroom

bulletin board

bulletin board

bulletin board

window

Teacher Desk

sink

cabinet

X electrical outlets

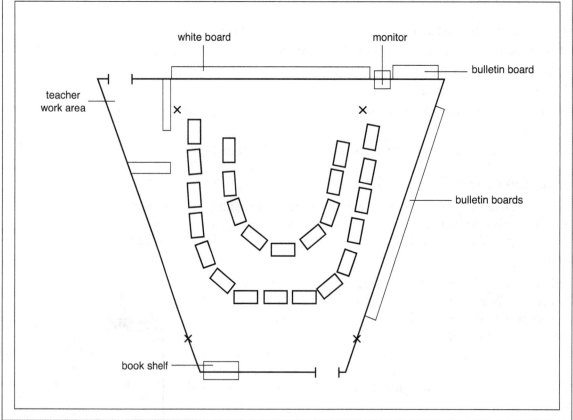

white board

monitor

bulletin board

teacher work area

bulletin boards

book shelf

Sample Classroom Floor Plans

BULLETIN BOARDS CHECKLIST

All Year

_____ Calendar

_____ Weekly Assignment Calendar

_____ Class/School Schedule

_____ Student Work

_____ Student Birthdays

_____ Classroom Expectations

Instructional

_____ Curriculum Charts

_____ Current Events—local campus,

local community, state,

national and international

_____ Instructional Unit Displays

_____ Weather Charts

_____ Compass Direction Chart

Seasonal/Special Events

_____ Seasons

_____ Beginning/closing of year

_____ Open House

_____ Holidays

_____ Student Self-Portraits

Functional Bulletin Boards

_____ Discipline Plan

_____ Classroom Assistants Chart

_____ Center Rotation Chart

_____ Lunch Count/Attendance Chart

Teacher Work Space Bulletin Board

_____ Emergency Information

_____ Alternative School Schedules

_____ Menus

_____ Duty Schedules

Example: Self-Portraits Many teachers begin the year by taking pictures of their students on the first day of school. They use a digital camera and process pictures on the computer or develop at a one-hour photo lab so the pictures are ready by the second day of school. Students are then given their photo and an 8″ X 11″ piece of paper or are directed to input their photos into a document on the computer. Students design their page with their picture and name, and identify skills, talents, hobbies, friends, and family. Students then share their "self-portrait," either with the whole class or with their working groups. Their artwork can be displayed. Students and teachers enjoy getting to know each other. In addition, the pictures help make the classroom a shared learning environment.

Example: Attendance/Lunch Count Chart As the students enter the room, they routinely take their attendance and signal their choice for lunch by placing a different colored and labeled Popsicle stick in their name pocket located on the attendance chart. For example, a white stick means the student has brought lunch and will only need to purchase milk. A striped stick means the student will purchase a hot meal, and the dotted stick means the student will purchase a salad bar lunch. If a lunch stick is not in the name pocket, it means the student is absent. The attendance assistant simply counts the different types of sticks and completes the lunch form while the teacher completes the attendance slip.

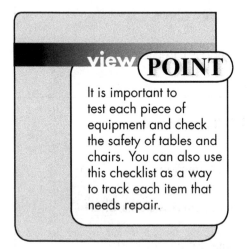

view **POINT**

It is important to test each piece of equipment and check the safety of tables and chairs. You can also use this checklist as a way to track each item that needs repair.

DETERMINING CLASSROOM EQUIPMENT AND MATERIAL

Teachers often walk into empty rooms when they are given a new teaching assignment. If this is the case, you will need to begin the process of ordering or locating supplies immediately. Others inherit a room from a teacher who has left everything to the next occupant. In either case, the following inventory will help you determine your classroom needs. Contact the administrative assistant or building manager for guidance in ordering supplies and equipment.

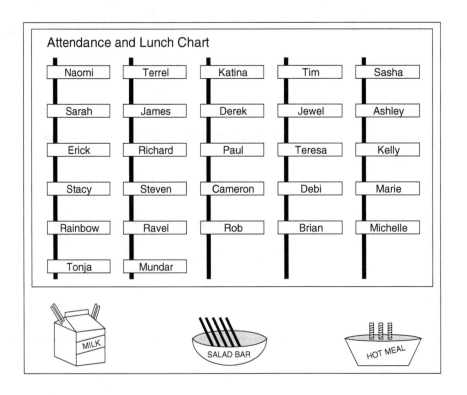

Attendance and Lunch Chart

Naomi	Terrel	Katina	Tim	Sasha
Sarah	James	Derek	Jewel	Ashley
Erick	Richard	Paul	Teresa	Kelly
Stacy	Steven	Cameron	Debi	Marie
Rainbow	Ravel	Rob	Brian	Michelle
Tonja	Mundar			

MILK   SALAD BAR   HOT MEAL

CLASSROOM CHECKLIST

Classroom Furniture Equipment

_____ Teacher desk and chair

_____ Student desks and chairs

_____ Tables

_____ File cabinet

_____ Storage cabinet

_____ Computer

_____ Classroom monitor

Classroom Materials

_____ Teacher editions

_____ Student texts

_____ Maps

_____ Globe

_____ Subject equipment

_____ Subject materials

File Cabinet

_____ Hanging folders

_____ File folders

_____ Index tabs

Storage Cabinet

_____ Whiteboard markers/eraser

_____ Paper cutter

_____ Bulletin board supplies

_____ Cleaning supplies

Audio-Visual Equipment

_____ Smartboard

_____ Overhead projector

_____ DVD/CD player

_____ Computer

_____ Adaptive devices

_____ Extension cord

Teacher's Desk

_____ Scissors

_____ Stapler, staples, staple remover

_____ Scotch tape and masking tape

_____ Pens, pencils, markers, crayons

_____ Post-its, note pads, note paper

_____ Dictionary

_____ Ruler

_____ Assorted tools

_____ Glue, glue stick, rubber cement

_____ Thank you notes and cards

_____ Postage stamps

School forms:

_____ Attendance

_____ Nurse referrals

_____ Hall passes

_____ Paper punches

_____ Ziploc bags (assorted sizes)

_____ Safety pins

_____ Health kit

CONTENT AREA CHECKLIST

Math Manipulatives

_____ Rulers and tape measures
_____ Measuring cups and spoons
_____ Clocks
_____ Number lines
_____ Age-appropriate math games
_____ Thermometers
_____ Meter/yard stick
_____ Graph paper
_____ Pattern cubes
_____ Beads
_____ Weights, balance, scales
_____ Play coins and money
_____ Flannel boards and felt pieces

Science Equipment

_____ Cage/aquarium for class pets
_____ Prisms
_____ Eye dropper
_____ Compasses
_____ Telescope
_____ Batteries/copper wire
_____ Rock sets
_____ Planting trays
_____ Rock/fossil/insect collections
_____ Magnets/iron filings
_____ Cooking equipment
_____ Microscope/magnifying glass

Reading/Language Arts

_____ Charts
_____ Paperback books
_____ Big books
_____ Dictionaries
_____ Thesaurus
_____ Grammar/formatting resources
_____ Writing paper
_____ Pens, pencils, markers

Social Studies

_____ Globes
_____ U.S. and world maps
_____ City and road maps
_____ Travel posters
_____ Community sets
_____ Historical photographs
_____ Timelines

Music

_____ CDs
_____ CD player
_____ Listening earphones
_____ Autoharp
_____ Bells
_____ Percussion sticks
_____ Flute-a-phones
_____ Drum

Art

_____ Markers and crayons
_____ Paints and brushes
_____ Watercolor sets
_____ Reference materials
_____ Portfolios
_____ Easels
_____ Smocks
_____ Paper
_____ Clay
_____ Yarn

Physical Education

_____ Balls of all types
_____ Jump ropes
_____ Hula hoops
_____ Safety Equipment

Technology

_____ Computer
_____ Software
_____ Paper
_____ Refill Supplies

In addition to basic classroom supplies, you need to know how to locate specific instructional resources that are available through the district. Most districts have a media or curriculum center that is a repository for materials that are shared across schools. The district media or curriculum center usually offers a range of instructional videos, computer software, CD-ROM discs for every subject that is taught. Ask district staff development personnel for a brief tour of this facility. You will also want to learn how to check out instructional materials and equipment, and inquire about the length of time materials can be loaned. After you have reviewed the district's resources, consider other sources of material, such as discount teacher supply companies that will send catalogs of their merchandise.

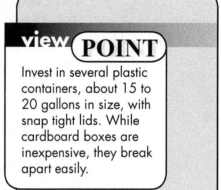

viewPOINT

Invest in several plastic containers, about 15 to 20 gallons in size, with snap tight lids. While cardboard boxes are inexpensive, they break apart easily.

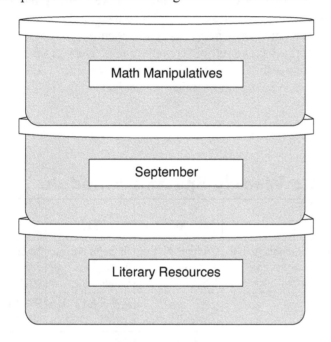

Math Manipulatives

September

Literary Resources

viewPOINT

Create a reference list of classroom supplies and their location.

Planning System

SCHEDULING

Management of time is essential. The first step in using your time wisely is knowing how much instructional time is available. Using a planning book, design your schedule. Be sure to set aside time for daily reflection and preparation. Obtain the most up-to-date school calendar from the school office. Note the following dates in your working calendar:

- New teacher orientation
- First day of school
- Grading periods
- Early release days
- Parent-teacher conferences
- Professional in-service days
- Last day of school

- School vacations:
  - Labor Day
  - Religious Holidays
  - Fall Break
  - Veteran's Day
  - Thanksgiving
  - Winter Break
  - Martin Luther King, Jr. Day
  - Presidents' Day
  - Spring Break
  - Memorial Day

Likewise, you will also want to know the school's daily schedule. For example, all teachers need to know:

- When teachers are expected to begin/end the school day.
- When students arrive.
- When lunch is served.
- When the students are dismissed.
- When special schedules are implemented.

Elementary teachers need to outline weekly schedules to track special classes, such as library, PE, technology lab, music, and art. As you organize and manage instructional time, know when your class is scheduled to have morning recess and when you are expected to bring your class in from lunch recess. The following chart shows an example of one elementary teacher's schedule identifying specials and pull-outs. You will need to carefully plan multiple content-area delivery in the remaining time through review of state standard expectations for your specific grade level. Also consider pairing with a grade level team member to share teaching loads in areas of content expertise.

Sample Weekly Specials Schedule

	M	T	W	TH	F
8^{30}	Students Arrive Instruction begins	Students Arrive Instruction begins	Students Arrive Instruction begins	Students Arrive Instruction begins	Students Arrive Instruction begins
9^{00}				9–9^{30} Art	9^{30} * Linda (Reading)
10^{00}	10–10^{30} Music		10–10^{30} Technology		
11^{00}				11^{00} * Erin (Speech)	
12^{00}	12–12^{30} Lunch	12–12^{30} Lunch	12–12^{30} Lunch	12–12^{30} Lunch	12–12^{30} Lunch
1^{00}			1^{00} * James (Resource)		Students Depart
2^{00}		2–2^{30} PE		2–2^{30} PE	
3^{00}	Students Depart	Students Depart	Students Depart	Students Depart	
4^{00}					
4^{45}					

*Special considerations: Beyond scheduling basics, most elementary teachers have students who require special education or language services where they are "pulled out" of the classroom for support. Design an appropriate schedule to collaborate with colleagues. This will enable you to cooperatively provide instructional assistance for those students in your class.

RECORD KEEPING

Student Codes Student code numbers help organize students, grouping of students, and paperwork at all instructional levels.

- Set-Up
  - Alphabetize your class by last names.
  - Number your students on your alphabetized class roster.
  - The numbers you assign become the students' code numbers for the year.
  - Assign each student his/her code number and require it to be in the upper right-hand corner of all work. For example: Allan Adams #1, Alice Bonet #2. For a secondary classroom, identify period and alphabetical number. For example, Robert Ally, #1. 1 (1st period), or Sydney Kline, #3. 12 (3rd period).

- Uses
  - Missing Work—Before checking papers, quickly put them in numerical order (or have a student do it). Glance through papers—missing numbers equal missing work.
  - Filing/Recording Grades—It takes only moments to record and file alphabetized assignments.
  - Keeping Track of Books and Materials—Number all class sets of books and/or class tools, such as rulers, scissors, and computers. When distributing/assigning such items, match numbers to code numbers. When it is time to collect these materials, any losses will be attributed to the responsible students.
  - Grouping—The teacher is able to group students very quickly; for example, odd numbers make one team, even numbers the other, or numbers 1 through 6 may go to the Learning Resource Center.
  - Random Grouping, Assignments, Rotations—The teacher keeps a container holding numbered sticks or papers. When needed, draw a number out, lottery style. This can be used to give a random order for presenting reports and/or forming groups.

Attendance The year can be started on a supplemental attendance sheet until permanent rosters are printed and made available. Attendance in your district may be recorded on computer. Attendance records are required by the state for funding purposes, so be sure to know your responsibilities for recording and reporting. Attendance policies are often governed by state legislation and are usually quite similar across districts. If a student is missing school without a notified absence, the parents will need to be contacted immediately. Be sure to know your system and the timelines for reporting attendance.

Mentor Voices

➤ "Include students in the making of the classroom management rules."

Sample Record-Keeping Symbols

Absence	◹
Excused Absence	E ◹ A
Unexcused Absence	U ◹ A
Tardy	◺
Excused Tardy	E ◺
Unexcused Tardy	U ◺
Field trip, school activity, nurse's office	⊠
Suspension	S
Late entry (draw line *to date of entry*)	E
Withdraw (draw line *to end of semester*)	WD

■ © WizData, Inc. 2008. Used under license from Shutterstock, Inc.

STUDENT ATTENDANCE CHART

Month _____ Dates _____ Period _____

Names	M	T	W	Th	F		M	T	W	Th	F		M	T	W	Th	F		M	T	W	Th	F
1.																							
2.																							
3.																							
4.																							
5.																							
6.																							
7.																							
8.																							
9.																							
10.																							
11.																							
12.																							
13.																							
14.																							
15.																							
16.																							
17.																							
18.																							
19.																							
20.																							
21.																							
22.																							
23.																							
24.																							
25.																							
26.																							
27.																							
28.																							

Following is a sample attendance letter and related correspondence to a parent from a school principal and the attendance clerk.

Letter **Sample Attendance Correspondence**

Green Valley Hills School

October 1

Dear Mrs. Jones,

We have noted a high number of absences and tardies for Martin. Martin has a total of 10 absences and 12 tardies since the start of school in August. State law requires the school to advise parents once a student has reached 10 absences. We are also required to inform our District Attendance Officer whenever a child has 10 or more absences or tardies. The District Attendance Officer will be contacting you for a home visit. We are committed to a high-quality learning experience, and absences and tardies can impact your son's learning potential.

School starts at 7:40AM and arrival after 7:45AM is considered tardy. Remind Martin of the importance of arriving to school on time. If you have any questions or concerns, contact us.

Sincerely,

Kim Phifer

Kim Phifer
Principal

Shauna Wilbraham

Shauna Wilbraham
Attendance Clerk

view POINT

Excessive student absences are usually an indication that the parents are in need of guidance and support. In these cases, the school's social worker should be consulted.

Organizational Charts There may be specific classroom activities that you will want to document on a separate check-in form.

Sample Generic Daily Check-In Form

Activity <u>Homework</u>   Date <u>Week of Jan. 28</u>

Student Code	Name	M	T	W	Th	F	Notes
1	Alli	✓	✓		✓	✓	
2	Byron	✓	✓	✓	✓	✓	
3	Lisa		✓	✓	✓	✓	
4	Ethan	✓	✓	✓		✓	
5	Luke	✓	✓	✓	✓	✓	
6	Sheri	✓	✓	✓	✓	✓	
7	Louis	✓	✓	✓	✓	✓	
8	Matt	✓	✓	✓	✓		
9	Lyn	✓	✓	✓	✓	✓	
10	Haley	✓	✓	✓	✓	✓	
11	Sarah	✓	✓	✓	✓	✓	
12	Karen	✓		✓	✓	✓	
13	Michael	✓	✓	✓	✓	✓	
14	Aaron	✓	✓	✓	✓	✓	
15	Parker	✓	✓	✓	✓	✓	
16	Dante	✓	✓	✓		✓	
17	Madi	✓		✓	✓	✓	
18	Sam	✓		✓	✓	✓	
19	Taylor		✓	✓	✓	✓	
20	Jordan	✓	✓	✓	✓	✓	
21	Rebecca	✓	✓	✓	✓	✓	
22	Kristen	✓	✓		✓	✓	
23	Mikaela	✓	✓	✓	✓	✓	
24	Justin	✓	✓	✓	✓	✓	

GENERIC DAILY CHECK-IN FORM

Activity _____ Date _____

Student Code	Name	M	T	W	Th	F	Notes
1							
2							
3							
4							
5							
6							
7							
8							
9							
10							
11							
12							
13							
14							
15							
16							
17							
18							
19							
20							
21							
22							
23							
24							
25							
26							
27							
28							

Sometimes you will be collecting forms, money, and permission slips simultaneously. The multi-purpose chart is extremely helpful to keep track of multiple activities.

Sample Multi-Purpose Chart

Student Code	Name	Field Trip Permission Slip	Photo $	Parent Conference Form				Notes
1	Alli	✓	✓	✓				
2	Byron	✓		✓				
3	Lisa	✓	✓	✓				
4	Ethan	✓	✓	✓				
5	Luke	✓	✓					
6	Sheri	✓	✓	✓				
7	Louis		✓	✓				
8	Matt	✓	✓	✓				
9	Lyn	✓	✓	✓				
10	Haley	✓	✓	✓				
11	Sarah	✓	✓	✓				
12	Karen	✓	✓					
13	Michael	✓	✓	✓				
14	Aaron	✓	✓	✓				
15	Parker	✓	✓	✓				
16	Dante		✓	✓				
17	Madi	✓	✓	✓				
18	Sam	✓	✓	✓				
19	Taylor	✓		✓				
20	Jordan	✓	✓	✓				
21	Rebecca	✓	✓	✓				
22	Kristen	✓	✓	✓				
23	Mikaela	✓		✓				
24	Justin	✓	✓	✓				

MULTI-PURPOSE CHART								
Student Code	Name							Notes
1								
2								
3								
4								
5								
6								
7								
8								
9								
10								
11								
12								
13								
14								
15								
16								
17								
18								
19								
20								
21								
22								
23								
24								
25								
26								
27								
28								

WEEKLY ASSIGNMENT CALENDAR

Assignments for the Week of _____

Student Name _____

	Monday	Tuesday	Wednesday	Thursday	Friday
English					
Math					
Science					
Social Studies					
Specials/ Elective					
Specials/ Elective					
Specials/ Elective					
Notes					

Student Name _____ Class _____ Month _____

Monday	Tuesday	Wednesday	Thursday	Friday

TRANSPORTATION CHART

Bus Riders

_____
_____
_____
_____
_____
_____
_____
_____
_____

Walkers

_____
_____
_____
_____
_____
_____
_____
_____
_____

Picked Up

_____
_____
_____
_____
_____
_____
_____
_____
_____

After-School Care

_____
_____
_____
_____
_____
_____
_____
_____
_____

BIRTHDAY CHART

	Names	Birth Dates
January		
February		
March		
April		
May		
June		
July		
August		
September		
October		
November		
December		

Time Management

Managing Time Schedule your time into two separate areas: school and home. It is important to learn how to make the most of your time at school, minimizing time spent on school work at home. Balance is key.

Calendar Purchase a calendar. Record school and personal activities immediately and update daily. Carry your calendar with you. Block out planning time, reflection time, and personal and family time. Only use one calendar.

Mail Read through mail and e-mail at the end of the day. Throw away or delete junk mail. Record important dates and deadlines on your calendar immediately and file notice in time system for future reference. Respond to any requests immediately.

After School Establish an efficient after-school routine. Grade and file student work. Reflect, plan, and prepare materials for tomorrow.

> ### view POINT
>
> After you have taught the first assistants their jobs, they can be responsible for teaching the next person the details of that specific duty. This saves even more time.

Student Responsibilities

Many routine tasks are explicitly taught by the teacher. However, many daily routines, once taught should be maintained by the students in your class.

Determining Student Jobs Classroom jobs build ownership and pride in the classroom. Students enjoy assisting. The following is a list of possible classroom jobs. Select the jobs appropriate for your classroom and grade level.

- Attendance Taker
- Technology Assistant
- Homework Assistant
- Class Secretary
- Paper Passer

- Packet Makers
- Librarian
- Pencil Sharpener
- Assignment Assistant
- Study Buddy Monitor

- Lunch Chart Recorder
- Line Leader
- Errand Runners

Whatever jobs you decide to assign, be sure students complete their responsibilities. Specifically teach the job details.

© MWProductions 2008. Used under license from Shutterstock, Inc.

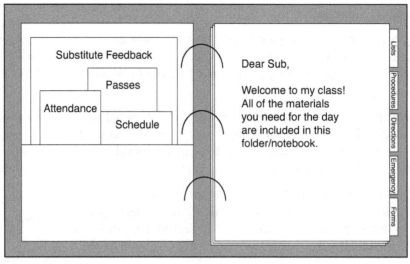

Sample Substitute Folder

Districts have policies and procedures regarding substitute teachers. Read your district handbook to determine:

- Whom to call to request a substitute.

- If you can specify a particular individual.

- To whom substitute teachers report.

SUBSTITUTE PLAN

Substitute Folder The purpose of developing a substitute folder is to assist the substitute teacher in providing a coherent, quality educational experience during your absence. A simple way to organize is to label a folder or a three-ring binder to hold lists and memos essential to your daily routine.

Charts, Lists and Schedules

- Seating chart/s.
- School schedule.
- Outline of your daily schedule.
- Special classes, times, and students affected.
- Special needs students.
- Names of teachers for assistance (including aide and resource teachers).
- List of parent volunteers (names, days, times).
- List of school personnel. See Who's Who on page 46.

Procedures

- Welcoming/opening the school day.
- Attendance.
- Classroom management/discipline.
- Specific instructional procedures.
- Restroom use.
- Student duties.

Directions

- Supplies and instructional material.
- School map.
- Special classes.
- Teachers' workroom/restroom.

Emergency Procedures

- Fire/bomb/earthquake drills
- School discipline code protocol
- Severe weather/rainy day schedule

Forms

- Discipline referrals
- Hall passes
- Learning Resource Center passes
- Nurse's office passes
- Guidance office passes

view POINT

At the end of each day, prepare for the possibility of a substitute the following day. Collect and organize teaching materials and place the sub folder on top. That way you are always ready for tomorrow, no matter what happens.

Substitute Follow-Up Many districts will ask you to evaluate the substitute teacher's performance. This information is used to determine who will be rehired to substitute at the school again. Include a substitute teacher evaluation form in your substitute folder.

PREPARING TO BE A SUBSTITUTE

Securing a Substitute Position One way to establish yourself as an excellent teacher candidate is to work as a substitute teacher. To apply for a substitute teaching position, contact the district personnel office. Districts use similar hiring procedures to employ substitutes. See page 48.

To increase your chances of being called to substitute, you may need to make contacts in numerous districts. Joining local teacher associations is one way to begin making connections. Another is to make an appointment to meet the principal or assistant principal at the schools where you wish to substitute. Before you meet with the appropriate administrator, it is wise to prepare yourself for the interview.

Common interview questions may include:

- What is your teaching experience?
- Why do you want to substitute teach?
- What are your long-term career goals?
- Are you willing to substitute on any day of the week?
- What would you do if there were no lesson plans?

view POINT

Always remind your students that you expect them to demonstrate respect and appropriate behavior whenever a substitute teacher is present.

WHO'S WHO

	Name	Phone Extension	E-mail
Principal	_____	_____	_____
Assistant Principal	_____	_____	_____
Guidance Counselor	_____	_____	_____
Secretary	_____	_____	_____
Nurse	_____	_____	_____
Custodian	_____	_____	_____
Grade Level/Department	_____	_____	_____

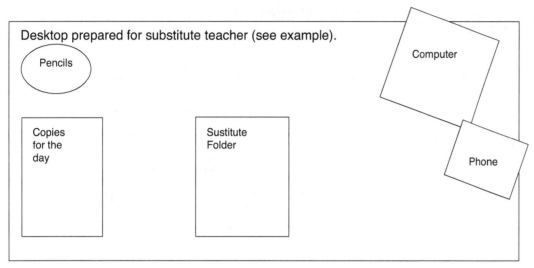

Desktop prepared for substitute teacher (see example).

Pencils

Computer

Copies for the day

Sustitute Folder

Phone

▬▬ Desktop prepared for substitute teacher (see example).

Also, think of questions that you may want to ask the interviewer:

- Does the school have a substitute-training program?
- Are substitutes expected to attend faculty meetings?
- Do substitutes assume the extra duties that the teachers are assigned?
- What are the school/district discipline policies and procedures?

Being an Effective Substitute The first rule of subbing is to be prepared!

- When you get "the call," find out as much as possible about the grade, subjects, and school. It may be in the early hours of the morning. Keep a memo pad and pencil by your phone.
- Use the teacher's established classroom management system as much as possible.
- Bring extra supplies and materials.
- Connect with other teachers. Let them know you are interested in substituting for them in the future.
- Caution—Do not share any negative details about the classrooms of teachers for whom you substitute, even if other teachers ask leading questions.

Maintaining Your Position To maintain your position, you need to meet the expectations of administrators, teachers and students.

- Administrators want substitutes to:
  - Arrive on time.
  - Be in classrooms on time.
  - Take accurate attendance.
  - Maintain order.
  - Fulfill duties as assigned.

view **POINT**

When you meet with the appropriate administrator listen, question, and learn; bring your portfolio, and share your career goals. It will not be long before you receive calls to work as a substitute teacher.

SUBSTITUTE TEACHER EVALUATION FORM

Substitute Teacher's Name _____ Date_____

Phone _____ E-mail_____

Overall evaluation of student behavior:

Reluctant   Cooperative

1   2   3   4   5   6   7   8   9   10

List individuals who were supportive and describe their contribution.

_____

_____

_____

List individuals who were uncooperative or who behaved inappropriately, and describe their behavior and your follow-up.

_____

_____

_____

Highlights of student work.

_____

_____

_____

List any assignments you were unable to complete.

_____

_____

_____

Other comments:

_____

_____

_____

Include any work you collected with this form.

Thank you.

- Teachers want substitutes to:
  - Take attendance.
  - Follow the provided lesson plans.
  - Engage students in assigned activities.
  - Maintain a positive classroom culture.

- Students want the substitute to:
  - Engage them in meaningful learning.
  - Maintain consistency in classroom routines.

Learning While You Substitute Use the time you substitute as an opportunity to collect great teaching ideas.

- Bring a camera and take snapshots of creative bulletin boards.
- Document effective classroom management techniques.
- Make notes of interesting content-related activities.
- Talk to the teachers and gather more ideas.

Teaching Tricks: The Sub Bag Many classrooms are well equipped and organized. It is a joy to substitute for the classroom teacher. However, some classrooms are disorganized, and may not be well stocked with everyday necessities. It is hard to predict; so to be adequately prepared, bring a substitute bag. The bag might include:

- Selection of books and short stories suitable for the grades you are teaching;
- Quick, easy activities you can use to become familiar with the students;
- Sponge activities that students complete as you are taking attendance;
- Supplemental games or activities to use if there is time left in the day or class period;
- Generic lesson plans—primary, elementary and secondary;
- Blank transparencies and transparency pens;
- Selection of pencils, pens, markers, and crayons;
- Blank paper, both unlined and lined;
- Money for lunch or bring your own lunch;
- Change for the soft-drink machine.

An Effective Start

"What will I do on the first day of school?" This is a common question almost all students ask themselves. However, as you approach your first day of teaching a new class, you are probably asking yourself exactly the same question.

What you do on the first day of school sets the tone for your classroom. This is the first time the students will see you in action. Research shows that students make decisions about a teacher's effectiveness within the first few minutes of the first day of class. Fortunately, with thoughtful planning, the first days of school can be fun and academically successful for you and your students.

Wearing a collared school-logo or school-colored shirt immediately identifies to students that you are a faculty member.

How Do You Plan to Dress?

Dressing professionally models pride in your teaching position. However, what is considered professional dress may be somewhat different depending on the grade level you teach, school climate, and the larger community in which the school is located.

Present yourself to the students, parents, and colleagues in a comfortable, yet professional outfit. Wear clothing appropriate to daily scheduled activities and in accordance with school/district policy.

How Do You Plan to Welcome Your Students?

Your students need to feel welcome in your classroom. Some elementary teachers use student names to decorate their doors. Teachers might design and laminate unique name tags with sturdy strings to wear like necklaces, which may also be used throughout the year for field trips. These novelty nametags may help both teacher and students immediately recognize members of their class.

Smile! Enthusiastically greet your students. Your energy will motivate student learning and begin to build a positive classroom climate.

How Do You Plan to Assign Seating?

Assigning seats helps teachers begin to learn student names and provides the students with a sense of knowing there is a place in the room that belongs to them. Assigned seating:

- Facilitates attendance recording
- Helps the teacher call students by name
- Facilitates connecting names and faces.

Changing assigned seats routinely provides students the opportunity to build relationships, learn from others, and positively engage in the classroom dynamic. Leaving students in the same seating arrangements for extended periods of time can create management challenges.

© 2008 Jupiter Images Corporation, Inc.

Seating Assignment Example

It's in the Cards

A way to assign seating involves a random activity called "Matching Cards." To conduct this activity the teacher needs two decks of playing cards. With one deck of cards the teacher quickly tapes one card to each desk. When the students arrive, the teacher hands each student a card from the second deck. Students then find their seat by matching cards. The teacher can then use the cards as a quick grouping strategy; for instance, "I need all the diamonds to line up," or "All the Kings can work in a group." An "Old Maid" deck of cards may also be used.

As you begin to learn more about your students, you may need to adjust the seating arrangements. Students with behavioral, visual, or auditory challenges may need special considerations.

How Do You Plan to Introduce Yourself?

The first thing most students want to know is their teacher's name. In addition to writing your name on the board, you will want to introduce yourself.

Students of all ages enjoy knowing something personal about their teachers on the first day of school. Personal information helps students relate to their teacher, and reduces any anxieties. Be sure that any personal information you share about yourself is appropriate. You might share something about your family life, hobbies, or pets. In addition, students may appreciate hearing something about your professional background. Many teachers display pictures of themselves, their families, pets, and hobbies on a "Getting To Know You" bulletin board.

How Do You Plan to Begin to Know Your Students?

Posting class rosters will help students find the right classroom. Name tags will help you connect names and faces. But these first steps do not include you "getting to know" your students. Learning about your students is one of your most critical responsibilities, and includes discovering interests, talents and skills, becoming aware of home situations, and understanding unique learning styles.

Getting to know your students takes time and is not something that can be accomplished by the end of the first day of school. However, you can speed up this process by providing opportunities for students to get to know each other and learn about you. Students will enjoy introducing themselves by participating in one or more of the following activities.

"Getting-to-Know-You" Graphing Give each student a sticky note. Then give directions for students to identify what month and season their birthday falls in. For example, have students write their name and birthday month on the sticky and place it on the graph where it belongs.

> **view POINT**
>
> Have you considered how you will introduce the instructional assistants and/or the resource teachers who work with you? These individuals are an important part of your classroom community; their roles and responsibilities should be described also.

Spring (March, April, May)		Summer (June, July, August)		Fall (September, October, November)		Winter (December, January, February)	
Joey April	Lisa March	Sheri June	Jade Aug.	Dave Nov.	A. J. Nov.	Ali Dec.	Addi Jan.
Sarah April	Max May	Katie Aug.		Tara Oct.	Tami Sept.	Mark Jan.	Adam Dec.
Madi May	Jon March			Mike Nov.	Ana Nov.	Nikki Dec.	
Jose April	Jake April			Keri Sept.			

▬ Sample Birthday Season Graph

view POINT

Students find it exciting to eat lunch with their teachers and it gives the teacher an opportunity to get to know the students. Plan a weekly or biweekly "Eat with the Teacher" day.

Tasty Introductions Pass around a bag of M & Ms and ask students to take three. They cannot eat them. Once all the students have M & Ms, instruct them that for each M & M they have, they must say one thing about themselves. The teacher should model this activity; for example, the teacher takes three M & Ms and demonstrates by stating three things about herself:

1. I have a dog named Sasha.
2. I like to hike.
3. My favorite food is Italian.

At the end of the activity, share the rest of the M & Ms.

All Wound Up Start with a piece of yarn about two feet long. Give to one student. As the student winds the yarn loosely around their hand, he/she shares appropriate personal information. When the yarn is all used, they must stop talking and pass the piece of yarn to the next student. This technique encourages quiet students to share more than just their name, and subtly limits the amount of time some students could dominate the floor. The teacher should model this activity.

Pair Shares Split students into pairs. Each pair has one minute to find a couple things they have in common. At the end of the minute, put two pairs together and give the foursome a minute to find things they have in common. Finally, each group presents the list of things they have in common to the rest of the class. The teacher should model the type of information that is most appropriate; for instance:

- Favorite subject in school;
- Favorite kind of stories (mystery, biography, factual);
- Type of pet/s;
- Favorite television shows;
- Favorite movie.

Scavenger Hunt Give each student a scavenger hunt list to build relationships with classmates. See page 53 for a suggested scavenger hunt.

Interview Your Partner Give each student the interview sheet, found on page 54, to pair with a partner.

Learning About You Ask your students to provide information essential for you. A suggested format and questions are on page 55.

SCAVENGER HUNT

Find Someone Who:

Lived in another state_____

Speaks another language _____

Has more than two pets _____

Has visited Disneyland _____

Has more than three siblings _____

Is wearing more than two rings _____

Can do a cartwheel_____

Is named after a movie/TV star _____

Plays a sport_____

Plays a musical instrument _____

Wears the same size shoes that you wear_____

INTERVIEW YOUR PARTNER

Name _____ Date _____ Hour _____

Your assignment is to interview your partner. You will record your partner's answers on this sheet.

When you have finished interviewing your partner and writing down their answers, they will interview you.

There are several group skills I want you to practice while doing this. They are:

1. Be kind in your words and actions.

2. Use your partner's name and look at him/her while you are asking questions.

3. Wait for your partner to finish speaking before you continue.

Find out the following things about your partner:

Name _____ Birthday _____

Number of sisters _____ Number of brothers _____

Types of pets _____ Favorite sports team _____

Questions:

1. Who is your favorite song, musician or musical group?

2. What is your favorite movie?

3. What is your favorite type of pizza?

4. If you could have any one wish granted to improve the world for everyone, what would it be?

5. If you could go anywhere in the world to visit, where would it be and why?

6. What is one of your favorite memories?

LEARNING ABOUT YOU

Name _____ Age _____ Date of Birth _____

Parent/Guardian Names _____

Parents' Phone Numbers: Home _____ Work _____

                         _____   _____

Parents' Employment _____

1. How do you get to and from school?

2. List the names and ages of your brothers and sisters.

3. What language do you speak at home?

4. Do you have any health concerns I should know about?

5. Do you have access to a computer? If so, do you have e-mail we can use to communicate?

6. What activities/hobbies/sports do you enjoy the most?

7. What activities do you least enjoy?

8. What are your favorite TV shows?

9. What are the titles of some of your favorite books?

10. What are your educational goals for this year?

11. What other things would you like me to know about you?

WHAT DO YOU PLAN TO TEACH?

Consider your day in small increments of time. A tight schedule encourages you to over-plan. This is important since you are responding to logistics, review materials, expectations, and new instruction.

Remember that a large part of your first day will revolve around meeting your students and establishing classroom routines and expectations. Your demeanor and expectations on this day will affect students' behavior for the entire year. Consider how you will:

- Meet students at the door;
- Greet students and introduce yourself;
- Have a prepared seating chart;
- Take attendance and ask students to clarify name pronunciation;
- Implement a get-acquainted activity;
- Discuss classroom policies;
- Teach procedures in context;
- Discuss the school-wide discipline plan;
- Conduct engaging and relevant content learning and activities to set the tone for the year;
- Issue textbooks;
- Establish a dismissal routine that emphasizes neatness and orderliness.

It is very important to schedule time during the first day for engaging students in real content work. This will give the students a look into what is to come, and something specific to communicate when their parents ask, "What did you learn today?"

best PRACTICES

In a study conducted by Garrahy, Cothran, and Kulinna, teachers reported that the two most common sources of knowledge for classroom management included trial-and-error and experience with children. Their findings suggest that learning to manage one's classroom is an ongoing, developmental process influenced by personal and contextual forces.

- Teachers believed strongly in their wisdom of practice and the wisdom of their colleagues' practice.
- Teachers addressed the need for, and importance of, continued professional development.
- Teachers recognized the value in visiting other schools, the role of professional conferences, workshops, courses, and staying current in the professional literature as tactics for continually refining their management skills.

Garrahy, D.A., Cothran, D.J., & Kulinna, P.H. (2005, September/October). Voices from the trenches: An exploration of teachers' management knowledge. *The Journal of Educational Research, 99*(1), 56–62.

Questions for Reflection

evaluation QUESTIONS?

- How will you set up your classroom to accommodate organizational needs and student learning?
- What is your plan for an effective start to the school year?

CLASSROOM SET-UP
- How will you organize all materials to be ready before class begins?
- How will you arrange and organize your classroom?
- How will you set up your workspace?
- How will you decide content to be included on bulletin boards?
- How will you plan for a substitute teacher?

AN EFFECTIVE START
- How will you assign seats?
- How will you introduce yourself?
- How will you learn about students' interests?
- How will you learn about students' health concerns?
- How will you involve parents in the classroom?
- How will you give students a time schedule for the day's events?

Student Behavior

> "It is better to keep children to their duty by a sense of honor and by kindness than by fear."
>
> —BROTHER TERENCE I

Management Models

THE DISCIPLINE AND MANAGEMENT CONTINUUM

The following discipline continuum, chart and corresponding narratives provide a brief outline of philosophies and models associated with behavior management. These all have underlying psychological theories associated with their belief about people and behavior. Schools and districts have discipline and management policies and some school systems adopt a uniform model for their schools. These come in the form of adopting one particular model, a spin-off of one of these models, or a "make your own" approach. You will want to check with your school and district to review their management philosophy and practice. You will need to define your role in implementing that system. You will also need to make many choices within the context of your classroom for implementing strategies to work effectively with students and their behavior. Knowing your current stance along this spectrum will also help you articulate your practice and share with students, parents, colleagues and administrators.

Teacher-directed .... **Student-directed**

Behavior Analysis (Skinner)	Assertive Discipline (Canter)	Positive Discipline Model (Jones)	Social Discipline Model (Dreikurs)	Array Management Model (Kortman)	Choice Theory (Glasser)	Teacher Effectiveness (Gordon)

	Description	Role of Teacher	Implementation	Emphasis
Behavior Analysis (derived from learning theory of Skinner)	Observable behavior is changed by the systematic application of behavior modification techniques.	Arrange consequences and control conditions to reinforce good behavior and punish bad behavior.	Target the behavior for change; shape, model and use reinforcers and punishment.	The behavior is treated as the problem, not as a symptom of a problem.
Assertive Discipline (Canter)	Assertiveness training is applied with verbal assertiveness and rewards and punishments.	Assertively insist that students behave properly and follow through with a well-organized procedure when they do not behave.	Establish a discipline plan with specified rules, and use a check system with a hierarchy of teacher-supplied consequences to match student behavior.	The misbehavior is dealt with quickly and the teacher returns to teaching objectives, giving strength to corrective control.
Positive Discipline Model (Jones)	With the goal of increasing student engagement time and decreasing lost instructional time, an incentive process is utilized to help students support their own self-control and be influenced by peer pressure.	Provide a structured classroom and use body language, incentive systems, and individual assistance.	Use limit setting, responsibility training, back-up systems, and omission training within an incentive program.	Increased time on-task is the goal in the classroom.
Social Discipline Model (Dreikurs)	Emphasis is on equality, respect, cooperation, self-discipline and encouragement. People are capable of changing and human problems are interpersonal and socially embedded.	Provide a relationship with the students based on trust and respect, and identify one of four mistaken goals exhibited by a child when a problem arises, and respond accordingly.	Offer democratic classroom where students help determine rules and suffer the logical consequences of their own misbehaviors.	In a preventive and supportive way, meet the students' needs to belong in the dynamic of a class group seen as a social entity.
Array Management Model (Kortman)	Components of self-management and encouragement are incorporated in this model that focuses on situational variables and internal motivators that influence individual choices.	Orchestrate the class by providing a variety of choices in learning and interacting in an atmosphere that capitalizes on individual strengths and interaction styles.	Use proactive strategies for inviting all students to function in a cooperative mode. Consequences and identifying replacement behaviors are key components to corrective management.	Each person is self-managed. Teacher and students are encouraged to remain in positive and productive behavior, capitalizing on strengths in interacting and learning.
Choice Theory (Glasser)	Quality work of the students is the focal point for a preventive management strategy.	Be a lead manager who stimulates, provides help to students, demonstrates ways work can be done, emphasizes student evaluation of their own work.	Provide an environment to help students make good choices about quality work; have class meetings and individual plans to redirect students when misbehavior occurs.	School needs to be a good place. Focus on skills that apply to life and the use of problem-solving as the basis for making good choices.
Teacher Effectiveness Training (Gordon)	Self-concept and emotional development are the basis for this communication-based model, which uses active listening, I-messages and conflict resolution.	As a supportive and noncritical facilitator, help students identify and solve their own problems, emphasizing the relationship between the students and teacher.	Identify areas for acceptable and unacceptable behaviors; give ownership to who owns the problem and utilize strategies for each possibility.	Students control their own behavior through problem-solving and the teacher is a facilitator for growth.

Adapted from Kortman, 1996

Behavior Analysis

Description Observable behavior is changed by the systematic application of behavior modification techniques. Skinner examined the effects of stimuli on learning when stimuli occurred after a response or act. Two general conclusions were made that form the basis for managing behavior from this approach: behaviors followed by rewards are likely to be repeated, and aversive stimuli or punishment following a behavior discourages a response from recurring.

Role of Teacher Arrange consequences and control conditions to reinforce good behavior and punish bad behavior.

Implementation Target the behavior for change. Shape the behavior systematically in gradual successive approximations toward the goal. Deliver or withhold reinforcement. Use positive reinforcement, negative reinforcement, and punishment to shape behavior. Model behavior that you want to increase.

Emphasis The behavior is treated as the problem, not as a symptom of a problem.

Assertive Discipline

Description Assertiveness training is applied with verbal assertiveness and rewards and punishments. The focus is on eliminating discipline problems. The Canters have applied assertiveness training concepts and common elements of behavior analysis to create this model. The model has been described as a combination of behavioral psychology and traditional authoritarianism.

Role of Teacher Assertively insist that students behave properly, and follow through with a well-organized procedure when they do not behave.

Implementation Establish a discipline plan with specified rules and use a check system with a hierarchy of teacher-supplied consequences to match degrees of student behavior. Misbehavior prompts a warning and a name written on the board or in a record book and a series of checks given to specify pre-determined consequences. Teacher meets his or her needs first and then acts in the best interest of the students. Apply discipline fairly and uniformly to all students. Be firm, calm, and assertive. Students must be taught to be compliant. Positive reinforcement comes in the form of praise and tangible rewards.

Emphasis Deal with the misbehavior quickly and return to teaching objectives, giving strength to corrective control.

Positive Discipline Model

Description With the goal of increasing student engagement time and decreasing lost instructional time, an incentive process is utilized to help students support their own self-control and be influenced by peer pressure. This model is derived from Jones' studies on teacher effectiveness in motivation, behavior management, and instruction. The theoretical basis draws from behavior modification, neurobiology, and proximity research from anthropology.

Role of Teacher Provide a structured classroom, use body language, incentive systems, and individual assistance.

Implementation Use teacher-controllable skill areas of limit setting, responsibility training, back-up systems, and omission training within an incentive program. The value is to work first, then play. Provide incentives for accomplishing work. The student controls the behavior, with the aid of peer pressure. Intensify gradually

> ## Mentor Voices
>
> ➤ "Be prepared. Planning affects discipline. If every minute is used wisely, then interest is generated and problems are lessened."

specific verbal and nonverbal responses to respond to misbehavior. Have a defined structure in the classroom environment that gives students a sense of predictability, and includes teacher proximity to the students.

Emphasis Increase time on-task in the classroom.

Social Discipline Model

Description Emphasis is on equality, respect, cooperation, self-discipline, and encouragement. The underlying premise is Adlerian social psychology. The model focuses on the belief that people are capable of changing, and human problems are interpersonal and socially embedded. Dreikurs emphasizes the motivations behind behavior and the importance of school being a place where students experience acceptance.

Role of Teacher Provide a relationship with the students based on trust and respect, and identify one of four mistaken goals exhibited by a child when a problem arises and respond accordingly.

Implementation Offer democratic classroom where students help determine rules, are motivated by intrinsic benefits, and suffer the logical consequences of their own misbehaviors. Develop a relationship with the students based on dignity and respect. Use encouragement focusing on the process or effort, not praise which focuses on the person or product. Identify mistaken goals of attention-getting, power-seeking, revenge-seeking, or display of inadequacy. Help students through group discussions and group acceptance.

Emphasis In a preventive and supportive way, meet the students' needs to belong in the dynamic of a class group seen as a social entity.

Array Management Model

Description Components of self-management and encouragement are incorporated in this model that focuses on interaction styles and personal objectives in relationship to motivation and behavior. Situational variables and internal motivators influence individual choices. An emphasis is placed on both proactive and corrective behavior management. Both cooperative and reluctant behaviors are identified. Based on Knaupp's Array Interaction Model, Kortman emphasizes opportunities for students to capitalize on their strengths and a plan of action for replacing negative behavior with positive behavior.

Role of Teacher Orchestrate the class by providing a variety in learning and interacting within an atmosphere that capitalizes on individual strengths and interaction styles. For inappropriate behaviors, identify replacement behaviors, and if needed, consequences that bring students back into cooperative interactions and learning.

Implementation Use proactive strategies for inviting all students to function in a cooperative mode. Some of these include being responsive to student needs, teaching procedures, using variety in instruction and learning, positively reinforcing desired behaviors, and actively engaging students in their learning and behavior choices. Use corrective strategies for redirecting negative or nonproductive behavior. This includes identifying the replacement behavior and giving the student a choice to redirect behavior to the positive or have a logical consequence matched to the misbehavior. The goal through corrective management is to differentiate consequences based on student needs and bring students back to positive behavior.

Emphasis Each person is self-managed. Teacher and students are encouraged to contribute to a positive classroom culture, remain in positive and productive behavior, and capitalize on strengths in interacting and learning.

Choice Theory

Description Quality work of the students is the focal point for a preventive management strategy. Glasser emphasizes application of quality systems methods, combining the psychological model of reality therapy with Deming's theory as an industrial managerial theorist. The focus is on the "now" of the behavior and problem-solving is utilized to bring the class or an individual into quality work. The approach also stresses that basic human needs must be addressed by the schools.

Role of Teacher Be a lead manager who stimulates, provides help to students, demonstrates ways work can be done, and emphasizes student evaluation of their own work.

Implementation The school must help meet student basic needs of survival, belonging, power, fun, and freedom within the learning environment. Control theory states that behavior is a best attempt to get what is need-fulfilling. Provide an environment to help students make good choices about quality work. When misbehavior occurs, ask a series of questions: What do you want?; What are you doing to get what you want?; Is it working?; What should you be doing? Create an individual plan with the student. Routinely have class meetings to facilitate problem solving.

Emphasis School needs to be a good place. Focus on skills that apply to life and the use of problem-solving as the basis for making good choices.

Teacher Effectiveness Training

Description Self-concept and emotional development are the basis for this communication based model, which uses active listening, I-messages and conflict resolution. The humanistic ideology of the Teacher Effectiveness Training (T.E.T.) model of Gordon represents the Rogerian psychology, which views all people as inherently good and rational. Students are provided with communication skills to take responsibility for the problems they encounter or create.

Role of Teacher Supportive and noncritical facilitator helps students identify and solve their own problems, emphasizing the relationship between the students and teacher.

Implementation Identify areas for acceptable and unacceptable behaviors, give ownership to who owns the problem and utilize strategies for each possibility. Emphasize open and authentic communication. Emphasize individual differences and focus on inner feelings and thoughts, which lead a student to taking primary responsibility for self-control. Use the following essential elements with effective

communication: silently looking on, nondirective statements, questions, directive statements, reinforcement, modeling, physical intervention, and isolation. Use problem-solving.

Emphasis Students control their own behavior through problem-solving. The teacher is a facilitator for growth; the teacher uses the least control possible to understand the student.

THE ARRAY MANAGEMENT MODEL

Research has consistently shown that students learn more effectively and behave better in classrooms where personal and psychological needs are met. As you get to know your students, you will develop an understanding of their personality needs and interaction styles. This knowledge will help you proactively provide for varying needs and effectively resolve behavioral problems. The Array Management Model (Kortman, 1999), based on the Array Interaction Model (Knaupp, 1995), provides a way for you to orchestrate the management of your classroom by learning about your students' personalities and, in turn, helping you to understand why students behave as they do. Ultimately, this knowledge will help you respond to the unique needs of your students and provide a classroom community that equips students to self-manage in positive ways. This model incorporates many elements from various psychological models into a coherent plan to individualize behavior management to specific student needs.

UNDERSTANDING STUDENT PERSONALITY AND INTERACTION STYLES

The three most common interaction modes observed in the classroom setting are Cooperative, Marginal, and Reluctant. A person acting in a Cooperative interaction mode is positive, agreeable, helpful, and collaborative. The Marginal mode of interaction describes a person who is neutral in attitudes and disengaged in interactions. The Reluctant mode of interaction describes a student who is involved, but in a negative way. The following lists common behaviors observed when students are in either Cooperative or Reluctant behaviors.

Cooperative Behavior	Reluctant Behavior
■ asks questions	■ gets angry, verbally aggressive
■ works toward goals	■ demands perfection
■ initiates work	■ over-adapts
■ cares about others	■ draws attention to self
■ is enthusiastic	■ blames
■ interacts well with others	■ is disruptive
■ is attentive	■ withdraws
■ is eager to contribute	

Teacher and student personalities are critical elements in the classroom dynamic. The Array Interaction Model identifies four personality components called Personal Objectives. All people have all four components; however, one or two are more prominent, and tend to greatly influence the way a person sees the world and responds to it. A person whose primary Personal Objective is Harmony is feeling-oriented, and is caring and sensitive. A person with a primary Personal Objective of Production is organized, logical, and thinking-oriented. A person whose primary Personal Objective is Connection is enthusiastic, spontaneous, and action-oriented. A person whose primary Personal Objective is Status Quo is insightful, reflective, and observant. The following figure presents the Array Interaction Model descriptors, offers specific Cooperative and Reluctant behaviors from each Personal Objective, and addresses needs associated with each in a classroom setting.

ARRAY INTERACTION MODEL				
	Personal Objectives			
	Harmony	**Production**	**Connection**	**Status Quo**
Cooperative (Positive Behavior)	Caring Sensitive Nurturing Harmonizing	Logical Structured Organized Systematic	Spontaneous Creative Playful Enthusiastic	Quiet Imaginative Insightful Reflective
Reluctant (Negative Behavior)	Overadaptive Overpleasing Makes mistakes Cries or giggles Self-defeating	Overcritical Overworks Perfectionist Verbally attacks Demanding	Disruptive Blames Irresponsible Demands attention Defiant	Disengaging Withdrawn Delays Despondent Daydreams
Primary Way of Viewing World	Feeling-oriented	Thinking-oriented	Action-oriented	Observation-oriented
Psychological Needs	Friendships Sensory experience	Task completion Time schedule	Contact with people Fun activities	Alone time Stability
Ways to Meet Needs	Value their feelings Comfortable work place Pleasing learning environment Cozy corner Work with a friend	Value their ideas Incentives Rewards Leadership positions Schedules To-do lists	Value their activity Hands-on activities Group interaction Games Change in routine	Value their privacy Alone time Independent activities Specific directions Computer activities Routine tasks

Student Needs When you understand the behaviors and needs that drive each personality type, you can provide a variety of choices in your classroom that allow these needs to be met. When your students' needs are met, they will more likely respond with cooperative behaviors.

In a classroom setting, it works best to address all the students' needs in the classroom in a more global fashion by providing students a broad range of experiences, activities, and interactions. Remember, students can learn the same content in many ways. Carefully plan your week to alternate between direct teaching, group activities, paired work, and independent activities. Include higher-level processing activities, relaxing activities and upbeat activities that provide physical stimulation. By providing a variety in your instructional strategies and presentations throughout the day, the students will more likely stay in cooperative, positive behaviors. The following student scenarios provide examples.

Harmony Shanel is primarily Harmony. Most of the time she is sensitive and caring. Friends are important to her, and she often praises her friends or shares kind notes. She feels for other people and wants everyone to like her. She provides support for someone who is feeling badly.

© Lisa F. Young 2008. Used under license from Shutterstock, Inc.

When Shanel is in a Reluctant mode of interaction, she tends to overadapt, overplease and make mistakes on the most simple items. This often leads to a loss of self-confidence. She wants to please others so much that she loses sight of her own goals. At times she shows an attitude of helplessness, wanting to be rescued. As Shanel's teacher, you can encourage Cooperative behavior by addressing her areas of need. Value her special attributes and provide sensory experiences.

Harmony Needs

Value Special Attributes	Provide Sensory Experiences
■ Use comments like, "I appreciate the way you make everyone in the class feel welcomed." ■ Write a note on your stationary, letting her know you are glad she is in your class. ■ Ask to assist with another student who has been absent.	■ Create a comfortable working environment. ■ Allow water bottles or snacks, as appropriate. ■ Work with a friend.

What statement would be most encouraging for Shanel? Why?

a. Thank you for the way you are working.

b. Wow! Fantastic work! Your paper looked great.

c. Helping your group the way you did was kind of you.

Answer: c.

Production Marcus exhibits the Production Personal Objective strengths of being logical, structured, organized, and persistent. He is a thinker, a problem solver, likes information exchange and values such things as task completion, skill development, and schedules. He is full of ideas, and likes to share these with you and the class. He thrives on clear expectations and competition, and enjoys seeing his work displayed. He appreciates printouts and postings showing his progress and achievement. He is efficient and his approach to assignments is organized. He wants to know the plan for the hour.

When Marcus is stressed and moves into negative behaviors, he can become bossy or critical of himself and others. He may make fun of a classmate's attempt at completing a task. He may put undue pressure on himself to do things perfectly and perceives that others are "having fun" while he is the only one working and being "responsible."

As Marcus' teacher, you can encourage him into Cooperative behavior by addressing his areas of need. Value his accomplishments and provide time schedules.

Production Needs

Acknowledge Accomplishment and Work	Provide Time Schedule
■ Verbally acknowledge skills. ■ Value thinking by asking for input. ■ Provide leadership position or job.	■ Announce changes to daily calendar. ■ Have posted schedule. ■ Follow established routines.

What statement would be most encouraging for Marcus? Why?

a. Your presentation was organized and showed evidence of your research.

b. You're doing terrific . . . that makes me happy.

c. I didn't grade the math papers, so they will not count toward your point totals.

Answer: a.

Connection Rosario is operating from the Connection Personal Objective. He enjoys activity and action, and comes into a room full of energy. He is friendly and bright-eyed. He connects with others in positive ways, and wants to be the center of attention. He likes loud music and drama, enjoys a good joke, and likes to do things on the spur of the moment. He is full of ideas and very creative. He often asks his teacher, "Could we do it 'this' way instead?" He unconsciously taps his pencil and makes clicking noises with his tongue when he's working.

When in a Reluctant mode, Rosario can be disruptive, annoying, and attention-seeking. When he does get in trouble, he blames. Nothing is ever his fault. His pencil tapping becomes loud and intentional. His tone can become sarcastic, and he can easily hurt other's feelings.

As Rosario's teacher, you can best encourage him to become Cooperative by addressing his areas of need. Value his need for contact and to have fun.

Provide Contact with Other People or the Environment	Have Fun
■ Use Think-Pair-Share. ■ Engage in group activity. ■ Write answers on individual whiteboards.	■ Allow class presentations in front of class. ■ Offer a variety of activities. ■ Consider unique or alternative ways to meet objectives.

What statement would be most encouraging for Rosario? Why?

a. You must be proud of the way you are working your mind.

b. Thumbs up on that one!

c. I appreciate the way you take pride in your work.

Answer: b.

Status Quo Kylie shows the Status Quo Personal Objective. She is very quiet and shows little expression. She doesn't volunteer answers but when asked to contribute, she is insightful. She prefers to work alone, enjoys working on the computer, and is excellent at complex tasks. Kylie enjoys sustained, silent reading when she can sit quietly in the class or library and delve into a good book.

When Kylie becomes stressed, she withdraws. As she disengages from the learning experiences, she may exhibit a blank stare. She has trouble completing tasks, especially when the learning opportunities are more diverse and open-ended. Unfortunately, she may go unnoticed because she so quietly withdraws, sometimes to a point of despondency.

As Kylie's teacher, you can best encourage her into Cooperative behavior by addressing her areas of need. Value her time and space, and provide stability.

Status Quo Needs

Provide Alone Time and/or Space	Provide Stability and Clear Directions
■ Engage in independent activity. ■ Provide routine tasks. ■ Allow private time in classroom.	■ Have set routines. ■ Give clear step-by-step directions. ■ Check progress frequently.

What statement would be most encouraging for Kylie? Why?

a. I like your smile.

b. Your essay reflects insightful details.

c. Cool hat!

Answer: b.

TEACHING STYLES

Knowing your own primary personality and Personal Objectives will also help you better understand the type of management and instructional style that is most natural for you. Your plan to include varying styles will help accommodate the diverse learning approaches of your students. There are four basic management and instructional styles that compliment the four Personal Objectives.

Inclusive The teacher fosters a sense of belonging by interacting in a nurturing and accepting way, valuing students' feelings and developing a community of learners in a safe and secure environment.

Example: "Thank you for giving ideas and working together with your group. The plants I brought today will help us understand how important their existence is for our ability to live on earth."

■ © PhotoCreate 2008. Used under license from Shutterstock, Inc.

ARRAY INTERACTION INVENTORY

Complete the following survey to help identify your primary and secondary Personal Objectives, the most natural ways you tend to respond to the world.

Directions:
- Rank-order the responses in rows below on a scale from 1 to 4 with **1 being "least like me"** to **4 being "most like me."**
- After you have ranked each row, add down each column.
- The column/s with the highest score/s shows your primary Personal Objective/s.

In your normal day-to-day life, you tend to be:

| Nurturing Sensitive Caring | | Logical Systematic Organized | | Spontaneous Creative Playful | | Quiet Insightful Reflective | |

In your normal day-to-day life, you tend to value:

| Harmony Relationships | | Work Time schedules | | Stimulation Having fun | | Reflection Having some time alone | |

In most settings, you are usually:

| Authentic Compassionate Harmonious | | Traditional Responsible Parental | | Active Opportunistic Spontaneous | | Inventive Competent Seeking | |

In most situations, you could be described as:

| Empathetic Communicative Devoted | | Practical Competitive Loyal | | Impetuous Impactful Daring | | Conceptual Knowledgeable Composed | |

You approach most tasks in a(n) _____ manner.

| Affectionate Inspirational Vivacious | | Conventional Orderly Concerned | | Courageous Adventurous Impulsive | | Rational Philosophical Complex | |

When things start to "not go your way" and you are tired and worn down, what might your responses be?

| Say "I'm sorry" Make mistakes Feel badly | | Overcontrol Become critical Take charge | | "It's not my fault" Manipulate Act out | | Withdraw Not talk Become indecisive | |

When you've "had a bad day" and you become frustrated, how might you respond?

| Overplease Cry Feel depressed | | Be perfectionistic Verbally attack Overwork | | Become physical Be irresponsible Demand attention | | Disengage Delay Daydream | |

Add score:				
	Harmony	Production	Connection	Status Quo

© Kortman, 2006, 1997

Informational The teacher encourages group participation and decision-making. There is interaction between teacher and students that is focused on gathering and processing information.

Example: "Today we are going to study the plant life in our region. Will you please turn to page 24 in your text? Let's discuss question number one together."

Interactive The teacher invites students to assume as much responsibility as they can handle. Students are encouraged to interact creatively with what is being learned.

Example: "Let's learn about plants today. What are some projects or assignments we can generate to help us learn about the plants in our state?"

Independent The teacher gives clear, concise directives; the teacher tells the students what to do and how to do it, then allows them to work independently.

Example: "Take out your science text, turn to page 24, and answer the first five questions in your journal."

The most effective teachers use all four styles at various times in their classrooms. It is important for you to capitalize on your styles of strength; however, keep in mind that a majority of students respond best to a higher concentration of the Informational and Inclusive styles.

Proactive Management

The vast majority of classroom management problems occur because the classroom teacher is not:

- organized or prepared;
- able to effectively focus group attention;
- providing meaningful instruction, clear directions and appropriate assignments;
- teaching a lesson that encourages active participation.

Planning, instruction, and management are dynamically intertwined, with each affecting the others. Proactive strategies are designed to prevent discipline problems while encouraging students to solve problems in socially acceptable ways, and to manage their own behavior. When the teacher clearly delineates the expectations and consequences, the students are then able to make choices about their own behavior and satisfy their needs for autonomy. Thus, proactive strategies communicate respect, responsibility, and accountability for both the teacher and the students.

Proactive strategies are interconnected with classroom management and directly relate to maintaining discipline in the classroom.

Proactive measures are used to prevent and minimize management challenges and set your students up for success in the classroom. It is your job as the teacher to set a tone of positive and encouraging interactions in your classroom. Your tone and demeanor basically determine how the students will respond to you. Teachers should also develop clear expectations and provide multiple opportunities for students to succeed. One way to facilitate student success is by highlighting behavior that is appropriate and desired. Since it takes a person four to seven times longer to process negative information than positive, keeping your comments focused on what you want to occur helps with communication and response time.

 ## Classroom Scenario

Plan Ahead

Ms. Jennings learned the value of long-term unit planning during her student teaching. She knew she had plenty of time to gather her resources, refine study guides, and prepare quizzes and tests. Now she only had to review the plan for daily lessons. The students were used to checking the calendar on the bulletin board for the materials, textbooks, and assignments they needed each day as they walked into the classroom. Then they looked to the front of the classroom where the objectives for the day's lesson were clearly posted. They liked knowing what to expect and it saved Ms. Jennings precious time, not to mention the agony of answering the usual questions, "What are we going to do today? Do we need our notebooks? Are you collecting homework? Will there be a quiz Friday?" Ms. Jennings said, *"When I plan well and teach according to my plan, I have fewer problems. Most of my kids get to class even when I know it is not their priority in life. I have many students who are basically on their own and having a rough time. They need a lot of structure, encouragement, and trust. When they begin to realize I do care about each of them, they step up to the task."*

 ## Classroom Scenario

Monitor Student Behavior and Class Interactions

After Mr. Johnson gave directions to the class, he walked around the tables of students. He noticed that several students were nearly finished defining and writing sentences with new vocabulary words based on meaning in context. Josh and Melissa, however, had not yet begun to work. Mr. Johnson commented, "Many of you are working diligently and are almost finished with your new words in the next chapter." He continued walking around the room. When he got to Josh and Mary, he calmly opened their books for them and, without saying a word, pointed to the words indicating they should start on the assignment. Both students got back on task without any further attention drawn to them or disrupting the class. Mr. Johnson reminded himself not to take their off-task behavior personally. He believes in having a clear set of rules and consequences, communicating them to the students verbally and in writing, and following through consistently. *"The saying, 'You can catch more flies with honey than with vinegar,' is really true,"* he said. *"Reinforcing positive behavior creates a much friendlier classroom. And I go home happy most days."*

© 2008 Jupiter Images Corporation, Inc.

First Days of School

- Getting acquainted activities
- Communicating expectations
- Teaching routines and procedures
- Teaching engaging lessons

Classroom Guidelines

- Behavior expectations
- Attendance procedures
- Tardy policies
- Make-up work and tests
- Grading scale, criteria, and rubrics
- Student responsibilities
- Safety considerations

Time Management

- Getting attention signal
- Maintaining attention
- Practicing routines
- Distributing/collecting materials
- Transitioning routine
- Pacing appropriately
- Ending the lesson routine

Maximizing On-Task Behavior

- Stimulating student interest
- Making learning relevant
- Linking to experiences

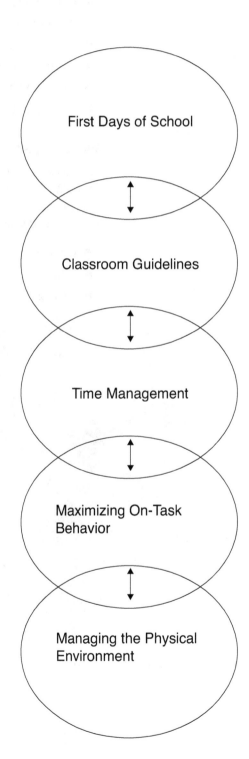

- Using effective questioning strategies
- Using student responses
- Guiding and monitoring practice
- Giving timely feedback
- Overlapping as necessary

Managing the Physical Environment

- Eliminating distracting noise
- Providing space for traffic patterns
- Adjust heating or cooling
- Shifting action zone
- Arranging boundaries and partitions to facilitate instructional strategies
- Arranging furniture and resources to accommodate instruction and safety

ESTABLISHING PROCEDURES AND ROUTINES

All classrooms have procedures and routine tasks that must be performed on a daily basis. Well-developed procedures become routines once established and serve as management tools, extend time on task and ensure a smooth functioning classroom. Recommended strategies for success:

- Identify effective daily routine tasks.
- Determine when to teach these routine tasks.
- Analyze each task and plan how it will be taught.

Experienced teachers and classroom-effectiveness researchers suggest that the establishment of these routines should begin on the first day and continue through at least the first two weeks of school. Classroom management experts stress that using this time to teach routines will actually give you more total teaching time during the year, plus the benefit of having a well-managed, organized classroom.

There are virtually dozens of routine tasks that could make your classroom more efficient and organized. The following list offers a number of routines and procedures that are used in effective classrooms. Many of these routines are described on the following pages. Identify the routines for implementation appropriate to your grade level and content.

ROUTINE TASKS CHECKLIST

Beginning Class

_____ Entering the Classroom

_____ Exiting the Classroom

_____ Attention Signal

_____ Attendance Procedures

_____ Lunch Count

_____ Tardy Students

_____ Sponge Activities

Grading and Checking Assignments

_____ Self-Checked Work

_____ Editing Checklist

_____ Grading Criteria/Rubrics

_____ Recording Grades

Classroom Management Procedures

_____ Rules of Respect

_____ Out-of-Room Policies

_____ Restroom Procedures

_____ Drinking Fountain

_____ Pencil Sharpening

_____ Fire/Earthquake/Bomb Threat Drills

_____ Noise Level

_____ Movement in Classroom

Work Expectations and Requirements

_____ Heading Papers

_____ Name/Number/Class Information

_____ Quality of Work

_____ Incomplete/Incorrect Work

_____ Turning in Completed Work

_____ Homework Check-in

_____ Missed Assignments

Instructional Activities

_____ Assignment Calendar

_____ Distributing Supplies

_____ Seeking Teacher Help

_____ Storing/Filing Work

_____ Computer Access

_____ Finishing Work Early

_____ Study Buddy System

Transitions and Dismissing Class

_____ Putting Away Supplies and Equipment

_____ Cleaning Up

_____ Going to Special Support Services, Speech and Resource

_____ Lining Up and Moving in Line

What Routines Will I Teach During the First Week of School? After you decide what routines you need, determine when you will teach them. It is important to teach procedures in context. For example, you teach lining-up procedures the first time you need to take your students out of the classroom.

The following chart provides a sample of the way one teacher taught the routines in her class. The second column is a place for you to outline your plan.

SAMPLE INITIAL PROCEDURES PLANNING CALENDAR	
Monday Attention Signal Lunch Count Routine Lining Up and Moving In Line Rules of Respect Entering/Exiting the Classroom End-of-Day Cleanup	
Tuesday Attendance Procedures Restroom Procedures Distributing Supplies Turning In Completed Work	
Wednesday Pencil Sharpening Drinking Fountain Noise Level	
Thursday Finishing Work Early Seeking Teacher Help Fire/Earthquake/Bomb Threat Drill Storing and Filing Work	
Friday Classroom Jobs Group Work Behavior Study Buddy System	

Monday

Tuesday

Wednesday

Thursday

Friday

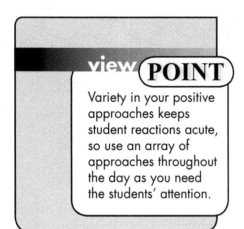
Gain and Keep Student Attention Gaining and keeping the attention of your students is critical to the smooth management of your class. Auditory cues are most effective for gaining attention because they allow students to remain actively engaged in an activity or assignment until they hear something that signals them to listen and prepares them for a change of routine or activities. Some effective approaches include using positive reinforcement phrasing, chimes, a rain stick, clapping, a music box, listening cues, writing cues, or whispering.

The following examples provide effective ways for teachers to gain and keep the attention of students. Choose the ones that are appropriate for the developmental level of your students.

Verbal Prompt Use a variety of verbal prompts to initiate attention, such as:

- Bring your voice down in volume to give directions;
- "Class, attention here please."

Be sure to teach your students when they hear these prompts, eyes on you and attentive to directions.

Take Five With this approach the teacher holds up five fingers and says, "Take Five." The students have been taught what five things they are expected to initiate when they hear and see that cue. For example: 1) Desk clear, 2) Seated at desk, 3) Hands in lap, 4) Mouth quiet, and 5) Eyes on teacher. The teacher can then continue by slowly counting down from 5 to 1, with everyone ready by 1.

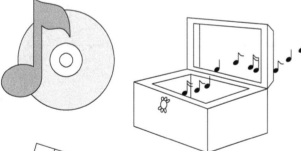

Music Box This technique encourages quick listening response and attention. Wind up the music box at the beginning of the week or record grade-appropriate song/s. When you play the music, the students know to be quiet and ready. When all the students are ready, shut the lid of the music box or stop the recording. At the end of the week, if there is any music left to be played, the students receive a pre-determined bonus.

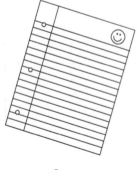

Writing Cue An example of a writing cue is: "If you're listening to me, you will put the name of the main character on the bottom left side of your paper." Every day change what you have the students put on the paper and where you have them place it. It becomes a game for them to listen. Be creative. It can be as simple as a smiling face or it can be reinforcement for something just learned.

Rhythmic Clapping The teacher can use clapping patterns to gain attention and signal response back from the students. The teacher claps a pattern and the students mimic the same pattern. This is continued until the majority of the class has joined in.

Rain Stick A rain stick can be hand-made or purchased at a nature store and has a soft, soothing tone that encourages a positive response in students of all ages.

RAIN STICK DIRECTIONS

Materials:

- wrapping paper tube
- 120 small straight sewing pins
- wood grain contact paper
- material scraps or suede squares (to cover ends of the rain stick)
- heavy-duty cord (to tie materials or suede to the ends)
- ½ cup dried rice
- ¼ cup dried lentils
- ¼ cup dried beans

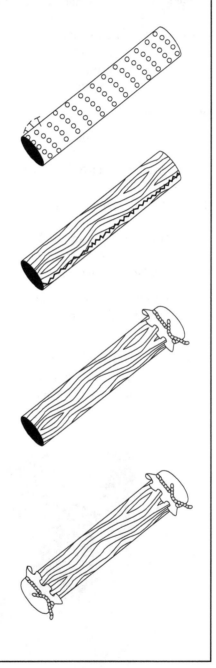

Directions:

1. Poke all 120 pins into the wrapping paper tube in a circular pattern. Make sure to stick the pin all the way through the tube. (You will leave these pins because they produce the "thinking" sound of the rain stick.)

2. Cover the tube and all of the ends of the pins with the contact paper.

3. Cover one end with the material or suede.

4. Fill tube with dry ingredients.

5. Cover the other end with your material and tie off to finish.

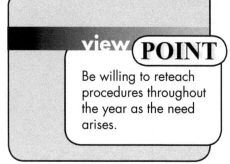

view POINT

Be willing to reteach procedures throughout the year as the need arises.

Task Analysis for Teaching Procedures After you have identified which procedures you need and when to teach them, you will need to analyze the procedure to decide how to teach it most efficiently.

1. What is the rationale of the procedure?

2. What are the logical steps needed to learn the procedure?

Following are examples of task analysis and explicit directions on how to teach the most basic procedures. Reminder: Procedures become routines only once they have been implemented and consistently used without prompting.

Attention Signal

1. What is the rationale of the procedure?

The teacher needs to be able to obtain students' attention quickly.

2. What are the logical steps needed to learn the procedure?

- **Information and Modeling**—*"When I need you to be quiet, I will ring the chime. When you hear the signal, you're to stop what you are doing, stop talking, and listen for directions."*

- **Guided Practice**—*"Let's practice. Talk to your neighbor for a minute."* [After a minute the teacher rings the chime.] *"Good, everyone has stopped talking and is listening for the next direction."*

- **Check for Understanding**—Observe the class as they learn the new procedure. Reteach immediately if there are misunderstandings. Initially, be sure you thank students for completing procedure successfully.

Exiting the Classroom

1. What is the rationale of the procedure?

   The teacher needs to know where all students are every moment of the day.

2. What are the logical steps needed to learn the procedure?

   - **Information and Modeling**—When a student needs to go to the restroom, special class, or run an errand, they need to go with a partner. They take their name clip from the class clip chart and place it beside their destination. When the students return to class, they replace their name clips on the class clip chart.

   - **Guided Practice**— *"Sarah needs to take a note to the office. Sarah, show the class what you need to do."* As Sarah models the procedure, the teacher narrates. The teacher will need to demonstrate this process multiple times.

   - **Check for Understanding**—Observe the class as they learn the new procedure. Reteach immediately if there are misunderstandings. Initially, be sure to thank students for completing procedure successfully.

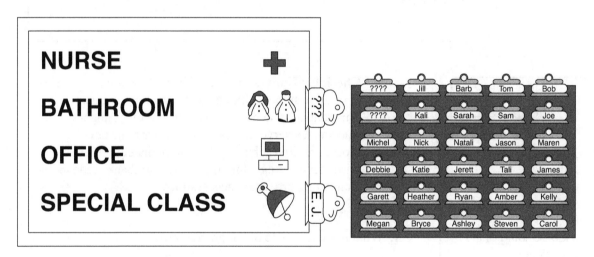

Lining Up and Moving In Line

1. What is the rationale of the procedure?

   Throughout the day teachers will need to quickly and safely transition their students to other classes and activities.

2. What are the logical steps needed to learn the procedure?

   - **Information and Modeling**—"When you line up, you need to stand and walk quietly behind the person in front of you. Listen, keep your hands by your sides, and watch where the line is going."

   - **Guided Practice**—"Everyone who is sitting at table one may line up. Let's see if table one can follow directions. Good, they got in line quickly but safely." The teacher will need to practice this procedure with all tables.

Lining-Up Examples

Line Up with Simon Says

There are many interesting ways to help your students get in a line. The following "Simon Says" ideas are both fun and help students listen carefully. Line up if you:

- Have a missing tooth.
- Are wearing a striped shirt, a blue shirt...
- Have a "B" in your name, a "D"...
- Are wearing sandals, tennis shoes.
- Have two (three, four, ten) people in your family.
- Own a dog, cat, bird, hamster...
- Have a birthday in May, June...
- Brought your library book back today.
- Have hair longer than your teacher, shorter than...
- Have blue eyes, green, brown, hazel...

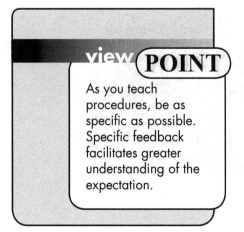

As you teach procedures, be as specific as possible. Specific feedback facilitates greater understanding of the expectation.

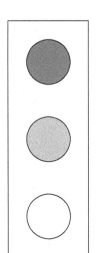

Red = no talking

Yellow = soft talking

Green = regular talking

- **Check for Understanding**—Teachers will need to observe students lining up and walking in line. This routine is somewhat challenging for younger students. Observe the class as they learn the new procedure. Reteach procedure immediately if there are misunderstandings. Initially, be sure to thank students for completing procedure successfully.

Noise Level

1. What is the rationale of the procedure?

   The students need to learn to adjust their volume in accordance with different activities.

2. What are the logical steps needed to learn the procedure?

   - **Information and Modeling**—The teacher will need to introduce the talk light. "When the talk light is set on red, you need to be completely quiet, not talking. When do you think the talk light should be on red?" Students and teacher generate a list of silent times. The teacher and students then discuss activities that are appropriate for the yellow light, which indicates time for soft talking. Students may practice soft talking to confirm the quality of that volume. Finally, the class discusses green light activities and volume.

   - **Guided Practice**—As the students get ready to do an activity, the teacher will ask, "How should we set the talk light?" The teacher confirms the volume level.

- **Check for Understanding**—Teachers will need to observe students as they work. If the volume is inappropriate, the teacher can comment, "Show me how you should talk when the talk light is set on yellow." Observe the class as they learn the new procedure. Re-teach procedure if there are misunderstandings. Initially, be sure to thank students for completing procedure successfully.

Pencil Sharpener

1. What is the rationale of the procedure?

   Students always have sharpened pencils available for use without disrupting class time.

2. What are the logical steps needed to learn the procedure?

   - **Information and Modeling**—The pencil sharpener collects the dull pencils and sharpens them during the last five minutes of class time. He/she places them in the pencil exchange can, points up.

   - **Guided Practice**—Students turn in dull pencils to pencil can and take a sharpened pencil. Pencil sharpener implements procedure.

   - **Check for Understanding**—Teacher will need to observe students using this routine. Reteach procedure if there are misunderstandings. Initially, be sure to thank students for completing procedure successfully.

Homework Check-in

1. What is the rationale of the procedure?

   Homework must be collected and sorted.

2. What are the logical steps needed to learn the procedure?

   - **Information and Modeling**—A student assistant sorts turned-in homework chronologically and/or alphabetically and places in assigned area.

   - **Guided Practice**—Students submit homework. The homework assistant implements procedure.

   - **Check for Understanding**—After the homework assistant has checked in assignments, the teacher periodically checks procedure. Reteach procedure if there are misunderstandings. Initially, be sure to thank students for completing procedure successfully.

Classroom Librarian

1. What is the rationale of the procedure?

   Librarian understands and implements classroom library checkout system.

2. What are the logical steps needed to learn the procedure?

- **Information and Modeling**—When students need to check out a book, music, etc. the librarian writes the students' names and book/music numbers on the previously created logout sheet. As needed, the classroom librarian records materials that have been returned to the classroom, and new materials to be checked out.

- **Guided Practice**—The classroom librarian assumes responsibility for monitoring the distribution and collection of these materials with the master numbered list and logout sheet.

- **Check for Understanding**—Librarian submits numbered book list and logout sheet to the teacher as requested.

POSITIVE REINFORCEMENT

Encouragement is the key to building student strengths. Following are examples of positive phrases that encourage students. Remember, positive phrases help students know what to do, while negative phrases are often confusing.

- "I appreciate the way Kristen is listening."
- "Taylor is ready to begin."
- "I am looking for eyes on me. Thank you, Jordan. Thank you, Maria."
- "I appreciate all the diligent workers I see."
- "You are really concentrating. Thank you."
- "There are many good thinkers in this room."

Other positive verbal cues include statements such as:

- "If you're listening to me, look at me and smile."
- "If you're ready for instructions, pick up your pencil."
- "If you're ready to begin, fold your hands."

Positive statements help produce an atmosphere that is uplifting and encouraging. When using positive statements with students, remember that the students are different in what they value as important. Some enjoy hearing how good they are at their work, others appreciate hearing that the teacher just enjoys having them in the class, and others are motivated by your enthusiasm. Although the positive reinforcement statements give you a starting point, remember that the most beneficial feedback is specific. Highlight specific aspects of academic work or specific behaviors for reinforcement.

view **POINT**

Consequences may stop a behavior, but positive reinforcement is more likely to change the behavior.

Positive reinforcement for one student can be perceived as a negative consequence for another. Have logical and natural consequences that match motivations for differing students. The chart below offers examples of possible reinforcements that would capitalize on the student's primary Personal Objective.

LOGOUT SHEET

Student Name	Item Description	Item Number	Check-out Date	Check-in Date

Procedure _____

1. What is the rationale of the procedure?

   _____

   _____

   _____

2. What are the logical steps needed to learn the procedure?

   • Information and Modeling

   _____

   _____

   _____

   • Guided Practice

   _____

   _____

   _____

   • Check for Understanding

   _____

   _____

   _____

Reinforcement Chart

	Harmony	Production	Connection	Status Quo
Positive Reinforcement	Work with friends Have stuffed animal	Receive award Post papers	Play a game Work with friends	Have alone time Work on computer independently

POSITIVE REINFORCEMENT STATEMENTS

- Thank you for the way you are listening.
- Thank you for the way you are working.
- You are right with me.
- You are thinking.
- That's the way to do it.
- You are doing first-class work.
- I bet you're proud of the way you're working.
- You are creating wonderful masterpieces.
- I like the way you are working your minds.
- You should feel good about your efforts.
- Wow! Fantastic work!
- Keep up the great work.
- You're doing beautifully.
- I can tell you take pride in your work.
- You are fabulous.
- You are showing great brainpower.
- You bring a wonderful feeling to our class.
- Thumbs up on that one!
- I like your smile.

STUDENT MOTIVATION

Keeping your students actively involved facilitates learning and actually makes classroom management easier.

Question and Response Techniques Help students keep their minds engaged and actively involved in the lesson.

- Ask a question first, then call on a student to respond.
- Give sufficient "wait time" for students to process their thinking before calling on someone for a response.
- Ask follow-up questions. Why? Can you tell me more? Give us an example.
- Ask clarifying questions. Can you tell us how you got your answer?
- Have students develop their own questions.
- Have a student give a summary of what has been learned in a lesson.
- Have methods for every student to participate. For instance:
  - Thumbs up or down.
  - Yes/No cards.
  - Individual dry erase boards.
  - Paired response.

© MWProductions 2008. Used under license from Shutterstock, Inc.

Think-Pair-Share Give the students something to think about individually. Then allow them to share their thinking with a neighbor. Then have a few students share with the whole class.

Variety New approaches and activities always excite and interest students. Some examples include:

- Provide variety in individual, partner and group activities;
- Use manipulatives;
- Use alternative learning methods such as drama, presentations and role-plays;
- Have groups of students teach various sections from a chapter or text; let them do added research and determine methods of presentation.

Corrective Management

Sometimes teachers and students have different ideas about the purpose of class. While teachers are concentrating on teaching and learning, students are often more interested in socializing and having fun. When such conflicts arise and preventive measures are not enough, the teacher must decide how to respond, and select a response that is appropriate for the misbehavior without jeopardizing the instruction or the dignity of the individual/s involved.

Classroom Scenario

Support Student Efforts for Self-Motivation

Ms. Kelly wanted all of her students to participate in the science fair but she knew she would have to work very hard to enlist Robert's cooperation. He did not want to work with other students or present anything in front of the class, not to mention the judges at the school. Ms. Kelly recalled that Robert's mother mentioned the family's interest in gecko lizards that her boys had been raising for several years. Indeed, the very reference to geckos sparked an interest for Robert. He said he had no idea that he could do something about his pets for the science fair. From that point on it was hard to get him to do his other schoolwork as his interest in researching, drawing, and writing about geckos absorbed his days and nights. Robert told Ms. Kelly some years later how that project changed his life. As a result of that science fair experience, he realized that he could talk with other students and in front of complete strangers about topics that interested him. It even initiated his college degree and career in working with animals at the local zoo. He told her that a good teacher is "someone who can hope for you until you can hope for yourself." Ms. Kelly believes that, "Each student is special and unique, and they all have special gifts to share. My job as a teacher is to discover those gifts and to celebrate them."

Being attentive to your students, moving among them, providing feedback continuously, and reinforcing signs of positive behavior allow you to immediately accommodate student needs before they spiral into negative behavior. When you first sense students slipping into marginal behavior, supportive measures allow you to give them a choice to come back into positive behavior. When students choose nonproductive behaviors despite your proactive and supportive attempts, it is time to step in with corrective measures. It is critical to set up a code of conduct with consequences so the students know what to expect when they make inappropriate choices. To be effective, you must be consistent in your delivery and response, yet flexible as you adjust to student differences.

Enforcing corrective discipline strategies is not as easy as it may first appear. In the past, new teachers were advised to use punitive measures, such as standing isolated in the corner or being left alone in a closet during time-out. Most experts agree these techniques did little to preserve the dignity of the student. In fact, research consistently indicates that negative consequences probably do more to instill feelings of worthlessness, anger, rejection, and rebellion, and lead to more negative behavior.

The goal is to help students learn to manage their own behavior. The perception of control is critical. Corrective discipline is often punitive and perceived by students as punishments given out by someone else in control. On the other hand, when students believe they are in control, they are much more willing to accept responsibility for their own behavior.

- Set expectations for your ability to teach without disruptions and maximize the students' right to learn.
- Clearly communicate rules and consequences; check for understanding.
- Decide whether misbehavior is minor or more serious; consider the context of the behavior.
- Use nonverbal or verbal interventions, or ignore minor incidents.
- Deal with the misbehavior with minimal disruption to instruction.
- Invoke the progressive consequence that matches the misbehavior.

- Preserve the dignity of the student; separate the character of student from the misbehavior.
- Follow through consistently; impose penalties calmly and quietly.
- Redirect misbehavior in positive directions.
- Encourage student to take responsibility for managing behavior.

view POINT

Check yourself: "Students, don't talk" vs. "Students, please be quiet." Videotape yourself. How often do you give students negative directives? How often do you offer affirmative guidance? Affirmative guidance shapes student behavior more quickly.

REPLACEMENT BEHAVIORS

The most important thing you can do as a teacher to eliminate negative behavior is to be able to identify what your expectations are in the positive. Sometimes merely identifying your expectations or asking a student to define what they should be doing helps replace their inappropriate behaviors with acceptable ones.

LOGICAL AND NATURAL CONSEQUENCES

The most effective guidelines or rules for the classroom encompass many concepts and behaviors in one positively stated phrase. As you discuss positively stated phrases, you are actually teaching your students. For example: "Show respect to all people and property."

Use logical consequences as your predominant corrective tool when students violate rules. You will see more sustained progress for appropriate and desired behavior choices. The initial investment will be well worth it.

NATURAL CONSEQUENCE

An outcome students experience as a natural result of their behavior.

Example: Adam blurts out answers.

Natural consequence—Other students become frustrated with Adam.

LOGICAL CONSEQUENCE

An outcome arranged by someone that is directly associated with the negative behavior choice.

Example: Adam blurts out answers.

Logical consequence—Teacher calls on a student with hand raised and does not acknowledge Adam's. If this level of consequence does not detour Adam's blurting, proceed to next logical consequence, such as isolation at side desk to complete behavior contract before re-entering classroom activity.

The chart below offers examples of possible consequences that would capitalize on student's primary Personal Objective.

Consequence Chart

	Harmony	Production	Connection	Status Quo
Consequences	Verbal redirection	Written contract	Loss of privilege	Behavior log

NOTICE THE DIFFERENCES: NEGATIVE AND POSITIVE CONSEQUENCES

Proactive/preventive redirection and appropriate, progressive, corrective discipline are effective strategies for managing students. Though many of us experience a great deal of negative consequences as students, it is positive reinforcement that has the greatest impact on student motivation, learning and behavior. Below are lists of positive reinforcers and negative consequences that can be implemented in your classroom.

Examples of Positive and Negative Consequences

Positive Reinforcers	Negative Consequence
■ notes, letters, affirmations to student	■ isolation
■ notes, letters, affirmations to parent	■ changing seats
■ leadership roles	■ sitting by teacher
■ changing to student-preferred seats	■ loss of privilege
■ assisting teacher	■ loss of group reward
■ individual or group privilege	■ time out
■ individual or group reward	■ loss of points
■ time to visit, do a preferred activity	■ cleaning room, board, campus
■ verbal praise	■ conflict resolution
■ displays of student work	■ behavior/academic contracts
■ membership on conflict resolution team	■ detention
■ independent learning contracts	■ Saturday detention
■ more time with assistance on projects	■ phone calls to parent
■ peer assistance teams	■ parent conferences
■ phone calls to parents with good news	■ principal conference
■ parent conference with student	■ class/school suspension
■ school awards	■ alternative classrooms/schools
■ lunch with the teacher or principal	■ gestures
■ donated books or magazines	■ ignoring
■ library or in-class reading time	■ home consequences
■ nonverbal affirmation	■ class discussions
■ games	
■ home rewards	

REDIRECTION TO POSITIVE CHOICES

A behavior contract provides an effective way for students to take responsibility of inappropriate behavior choices and plan for a positive change in their behavior.

REDIRECTION TO POSITIVE CHOICES: RESPONSIBILITY PLAN

My name is: _____

_____

The rule I broke:

My consequence:

My plan for change:

I can make responsible choices in the classroom. I will choose to control myself and help make this a productive place for myself and all the other students.

Student Signature _____

Teacher Signature _____

Date_____ Follow-Up_____

STUDENT CONTRACT

I, _____ agree to

By doing so, the effect will be _____

Student signature _____ Date _____

Teacher signature_____ Date _____

Parent signature _____ Date _____

Phone _____ Conference _____ Date _____

ANALYZING PATTERNS OF BEHAVIOR

Underlying Problems May Not Be School-Related Unfortunately, there are times when a student will continue to be disruptive or non-productive no matter what you do to make the lesson engaging, the activity relevant and the visual aids compelling. Sometimes a student has developed a failure pattern that is very difficult to modify or change. These failure patterns are often related to events and relationships outside of the school setting. Realize that the key for changing this behavior is consistency over time. Try your best to understand this student. Find consistent ways to reinforce positive behavior and set up consistent procedures to hold this student accountable for their negative behavior choices. Your positive persistence will eventually give you and the student a chance to celebrate the positive changes.

The following steps are effective for any student:

- Respect and value students;
- Develop and teach clear expectations;
- Provide choices in learning and interacting;
- Model positive behavior;
- Reinforce positive behavior;
- Consistently and calmly follow through with consequences.

The Student Is Not His Actions When a student has behaved inappropriately, separate the action from the student. Let the student know what specific behavior was unacceptable; help identify appropriate behaviors, then give the student an opportunity to make a change. Let the student know you believe in their ability to make good choices in the future.

© Rob Marmion Inc. 2008. Used under license from Shutterstock, Inc.

Ask the Students! When in doubt, initiate dialogue and let your students talk to you. Students will often give you cues for what they need to maintain positive behavior. These personalized interactions can often be the catalyst for significant changes in behavior. Use this time to create a behavior contract with the student. Putting a responsibility plan into writing provides important motivation for a change in behavior by providing accountability for misbehavior, identification of replacement behaviors, a plan for redirecting behavior and an emphasis on reinforcing positive behaviors. It also provides documentation for your records.

A Challenge Assessment The following checklist provides basic questions to guide you through a plan of action for developing clear expectations and consistent, logical consequences that are appropriate for each student. It also guides your reflections as you consider the interactions between student motivation and teacher behaviors.

CHECKLIST FOR A CHALLENGE

Plan of Action

- ❑ What is the plan of action for the student?

- ❑ Does the student know what to expect?

- ❑ What are the steps?

- ❑ What are the consequences for inappropriate behavior choices?

- ❑ How will I follow through?

Teacher Self-Check

- ❑ Am I consistent in my methods for follow-through?

- ❑ Was I well prepared for the class period and lesson?

- ❑ Did I have materials organized and ready for student use?

- ❑ Did I portray enthusiasm in my teaching?

- ❑ Did I provide a variety of activities?

- ❑ Did I have clear expectations? What were they?

- ❑ Did I provide clear directions? What were they?

Student Check

- ❑ Is this a first time problem for the student or a pattern of behavior?

- ❑ What other factors may have impacted the student's choice for negative behavior?

- ❑ Does there seem to be corresponding problems in the area of academics?

- ❑ Does there seem to be corresponding problems in the area of social interactions?

- ❑ Does there seem to be corresponding problems from outside the classroom?

Applications

CASE STUDIES

Part of becoming a good classroom manager and effective teacher involves experience in dealing with complex situations. Consider the following questions and apply them to each of the scenarios below.

- What will you do immediately? Why?
- Will you involve anyone else? Why?
- What other action will you take?
- What will you say?
- Will you report this to the principal? What about the parents?
- What effect will your actions and responses have upon misbehaving students, other students, custodian, principal, school, and you?
- What measures could possibly have prevented this incident?

Case Study 1

Josh, a student in your class, is quite docile. He socializes little with other students and never disrupts lessons. However, despite your best efforts, Josh will not answer questions when called on, do his assigned work, or participate in class discussions. He rarely completes assignments, quizzes, or tests. What preventive technique would you use? What is your rationale?

Case Study 2

James has been in a disruptive mood ever since arriving in class. He gets up, and on his way to the pencil sharpener, he bumps into Carl. Carl complains. James tells him loudly to "shut up." You tell James to return to his seat. He wheels around, swears loudly, and says angrily, "I'll go back when I'm good and ready." This is the third time such behavior has occurred. What corrective discipline strategy should you use?

Case Study 3

Before class starts, Audrey and Cindy are standing in the back of your classroom, talking. A few other students have arrived for class. You are standing in the doorway talking to the custodian. All of a sudden you hear shouting from the back of the room. As you turn, you see Cindy falling to the floor and Audrey grabbing a chair, getting ready to shove it toward Cindy. How will you respond? What school-wide policy would you need to follow?

Rodney has shown little interest in your class. He missed two class sessions this week, but he had an excuse from the coach. He was late to class by five minutes on three other occasions, but in each instance he had a written excuse from the nurse or another teacher. Yesterday, you needed to correct him for making faces and rude remarks to students giving speeches. Today, students were numbering off for group activities. When it was Rodney's turn, he was one of two students left that did not have a group. You pointed to the first student and said, "You're a one." You pointed to Rodney and said, "You're a two and I'll be a three. We can work together." Rodney made a face and said, "No way I'm gonna be in a group with the teacher." The class became silent. What strategies will you use to re-direct Rodney? Will you address him inside or outside class time?

QUESTIONS TO CONSIDER

Student discipline problems can vary significantly. The most profound usually require you to involve administration, parents, and, occasionally, external agencies, for example, the local police. Consider the following questions and sample answers on discipline and management issues.

What if students get into a physical fight in my classroom or on the campus? Loudly call them by name and, with a determined sense of urgency, command them to "stop now." Do not move in between the students unless you have the help of other adults. Instead, move toward them, repeating their names and the command to stop. Move other students away from the fight to secure their safety. Send someone for another teacher, a security person, or an administrator. If you have adult assistance and the students continue to fight even after commanded to stop, you have the right to intervene, or not to intervene, depending on the circumstances and potential harm to you.

Remain calm. Do not escalate the problem by reacting to verbal assaults, or provoke the students in any way. Be prepared to provide information regarding the incident to the administrator and parent/s in writing.

Support the decision of the administrator in the outcome and do not try to second-guess it. Most often, the administrator is acting on additional information, a history of discipline, and the safety of the individuals involved, even if one seemed more at fault than the other. Sometimes such an incident is referred to the police, for the welfare of the students involved and other students. Also, district policies can dictate police involvement.

What if a student brings a weapon to class or on campus? Obviously weapons, such as knives or guns, are illegal, but other items, such as sticks, chains, stars, nails may also be considered weapons. Determine the level of present danger to yourself and your students. At the lowest level of danger, ask the student to give you the weapon. Without escalating the situation or giving any explanation to the student, take it and put it in a secure place, or have another teacher watch your class while you either take it to the principal's office or call for Security to come and pick it up. In any case, do not return it to the student. Insist on a parent conference at the very least. Again, many district policies dictate law-enforcement involvement. If you fear for the safety of yourself and students, instruct the students to get down and lie flat on the ground, or seek shelter if it is available. Do not challenge the offending student. Make no demands, and listen to what the student says. Do not make any sudden movements. Protect innocent students to the best of your ability. Summon help in any subtle way. After such an incident, the students may need help in processing the incident, so be clear about the threatening behavior of the student and the appropriateness of your actions. Always document the incident.

What if a student threatens me verbally or with a gesture? Without escalating the situation or responding to the verbal assault, determine whether the student should remain in the classroom or not. Call for Security or send a student for help, if needed. In any case, report and document the incident to the principal. Threatening a teacher is against the law in most states; legal action may be taken.

What if a student riot develops out on the campus? Close your classroom door to secure the safety of your students. Some schools immediately lock building doors leading to classrooms. If you are outside, notify Security, police, and administration. Command students to stop shouting, throwing objects, or fighting. Protect yourself and students to the best of your ability. Render assistance as needed to other teachers, Security, and police. Follow directions. Go to the administration for further directions.

What if a parent becomes verbally abusive? Calmly and respectfully say that you are not willing to continue the discussion under the circumstances and that it will be rescheduled when an administrator can be present. The more intense the parent's verbal assault, the calmer you must be. Then leave or hang up the phone and report the incident to the principal immediately. Document the incident in writing.

What if I suspect physical, sexual, or emotional abuse of a student? You are obligated by law to report it to an administrator, who will then take the information to a school resource person or team, which is usually the nurse and a counselor. Based on the findings, a report must be made to Child Protective Services. If the child is in imminent danger, it should be determined what action should be taken. Under any circumstances, do not take action yourself, other than reporting to Child Protective Services.

What if a student asks me to promise not to reveal a confidence such as abuse? Explain to the student that, in their best interest, you will have to involve a school counselor. You are legally bound to report such incidents and cannot make such promises to students.

What if I suspect that a student is under the influence of alcohol or drugs? Do not accuse the student of being under the influence. Notify the nurse or an administrator to send for or accompany the student immediately to the nurse's office. Do not wait; you want the student to be seen in this present condition. The student's parents must be notified, and district policy must be implemented.

When should I send a student or ask that a student be taken to the principal or assistant principal? Immediately if the student's behavior presents a danger to himself or others. Otherwise, you must have exhausted all of the steps provided for in the school discipline plan, including contacting the parents.

What should I do if I am losing the battle in classroom discipline? Admit it to yourself, and the sooner the better. Seek the counsel of your mentor or a trusted colleague. Be prepared for the fact that behavior may get worse before it gets better as you begin to regain control, communicate expectations and tighten up on rules. If you do not have classroom guidelines, develop them, communicate them to the students verbally and in writing, and apply them consistently. Be prepared for some challenges. Continue to state your expectations and invoke consequences, positive and negative. Read professional texts and journals; see an instructional specialist, resource specialist, or other qualified person for guidance and direction; attend workshops, conferences, classes, and seminars available locally and nationally. Obtain videos and resources from the professional section in your school library.

What if discipline is generally a problem throughout the entire school? Work with the school principal to establish a representative committee to develop guidelines. Some schools involve students in tribunals and/or conflict resolution teams. School discipline programs supported by all faculty, staff, students, and parents are most effective.

What if a student's test conspicuously has the same right and wrong answers as another student seated in close proximity and it looks like cheating? What is your rule about cheating? Did you communicate it to the students? If so, then you are on firmer ground to proceed with questioning both students, one at a time privately. Unless you actually saw the cheating or one of the students confesses, you have little evidence and may only be able to provide a firm warning.

What if a student continually exhibits aggressive behavior? One student or another is coming to you daily complaining of his teasing, pushing, taking papers, and lack of cooperating on team activities. His parents are concerned but unable to bring about significant or lasting change, and feel at a loss.

Arrange a conference with the student, the counselor, parents, and yourself. At this time explain that you have exhausted all other avenues and the student has to regulate his own behavior. Set up a contingency contract for behavior and academics by involving everyone, using the following guidelines:

- Define the problem and check for understanding;
- Consider possible resolutions;
- Decide on one resolution;
- Identify steps for implementing the decision;
- Identify the consequences, both negative and positive;
- Student must agree to be in charge of monitoring the contract and report evidence to you and parent weekly;
- Ultimately, the student makes the choice along with the consequence.

Comprehensive Plan

Managing a classroom environment takes a comprehensive plan for both the teacher and the students. The rewards are worth the efforts. The gains include self-disciplined students in action and a positive and productive learning climate.

best PRACTICES

Marshall and Weisner found that, through implementing a system where students are taking responsibility of themselves and their actions, as well as engaging in ongoing self-reflection, students begin to internally motivate and are therefore more cooperative in the classroom. Three recommended practices include:

- Be positive;
- Allow students to have choices in their responses;
- Ask questions to effectively guide students to reflect and self-evaluate.

Marshall, M., & Weisner, K. (2004, March). Using a discipline system to promote learning. *Phi Delta Kappan, 85*(7), 498–507.

evaluation QUESTIONS

- How will you reinforce learning and behavioral expectations in the classroom?
- What strategies will you implement to develop self-directed students?

Questions for Reflection

PROACTIVE MANAGEMENT

- How will you align your management plan to school rules?
- How will you plan for emergency procedures?
- How will you build positive relationships with all students?
- How will you model positive attitudes, behaviors, and interactions?
- How will you encourage positive interactions from and among students?
- How will you reinforce positive behavior on a continual basis?
- How will you set clear expectations?
- How will you establish procedures?
- How will you identify classroom jobs?
- How will you use clear auditory cues for focusing and keeping group attention?

- How will you use positive phrasing?
- How will you provide engaging lessons?
- How will you include all students in class activities?
- How will you provide clear instructions for work and assignments?
- How will you provide multiple opportunities for students to succeed?
- How will you provide relevant learning choices?
- How will you understand varying Personal Objectives and student motivation for work and behavior?
- How will you provide for varying Personal Objectives/personality components?
- How will you use your knowledge of Cooperative, Marginal and Reluctant interaction styles?
- How will you understand and adapt to student needs?
- How will you value and respect students for who they are?
- How will you value work and accomplishments of students?
- How will you provide opportunities for contact with other students?
- How will you allow for independent work?
- How will you design your teaching to include varying management and instructional styles?
- How will you match your management philosophy to your teaching?

CORRECTIVE MANAGEMENT

- How will you adjust consequences to meet student needs?
- How will you consistently and calmly follow through with consequences?
- How will you utilize logical consequences for inappropriate behavior choices?
- How will you separate student actions from the student?

Reflection: Self-Assessment of Professional Growth

Name				Date	
Grade Level/Content Area					

Classroom Set-Up	Low				High
To what degree do I have the knowledge needed for setting up my classroom?	1 ☐	2 ☐	3 ☐	4 ☐	5 ☐
To what degree do I have the teaching skills needed for setting up my classroom?	1 ☐	2 ☐	3 ☐	4 ☐	5 ☐
An Effective Start	Low				High
To what degree do I have the knowledge needed for effectively starting the school year?	1 ☐	2 ☐	3 ☐	4 ☐	5 ☐
To what degree do I have the teaching skills needed for effectively starting the school year?	1 ☐	2 ☐	3 ☐	4 ☐	5 ☐
Proactive Management	Low				High
To what degree do I have the knowledge needed to create a successful proactive management plan?	1 ☐	2 ☐	3 ☐	4 ☐	5 ☐
To what degree do I have the teaching skills needed to implement a successful proactive management plan?	1 ☐	2 ☐	3 ☐	4 ☐	5 ☐
Corrective Management	Low				High
To what degree do I have the knowledge needed to create a corrective management plan?	1 ☐	2 ☐	3 ☐	4 ☐	5 ☐
To what degree do I have the teaching skills needed to implement a successful corrective management plan?	1 ☐	2 ☐	3 ☐	4 ☐	5 ☐

Next Steps

Set goals for next steps to implement best practices in the teaching standard of management.

_____

_____

_____

_____

_____

_____

_____

_____

_____

_____

_____

_____

_____

_____

_____

_____

_____

_____

_____

_____

Instructional Design and Instruction: Managing Student Learning

3

> **"** Command of scientific methods and systematized subject matter liberates individuals; it enables them to see new problems, devise new procedures, and in general, makes for diversification rather than for set uniformity.**"**
>
> —RENE DESCARTES

Effective teachers, from preschool through the university level, are able to connect with all the students in the class. They are also able to motivate their students and create an interest in learning, whether the ABC's or calculus. Research in teacher effectiveness has consistently demonstrated that when students are interested in a subject they usually perform better. Effective teachers are also incredibly good planners. They think ahead and deliberately plan for student success. Writing lesson plans is like planning a journey. If you expect to get where you want to go, you need to map your route carefully to make the most efficient use of time and resources. Likewise, teachers need to plan carefully to help students learn what is being taught, and how to make full use of opportunities to connect curriculum content and involve students in the learning process.

POINTS OF INQUIRY

- How do you organize lesson planning for effective instruction?
- How will you incorporate curriculum integration?
- How will you engage students in the learning process?
- How will you differentiate instruction to support student needs?

Lesson Planning

"The future belongs to those who prepare for it.**"**

—RALPH EMERSON

Planning for Effective Instruction

Basically, a lesson plan is a simple document that answers three questions:

1. What do you want students to know or do?
2. How will you teach the lesson?
3. How will you assess what students have learned?

During the process of answering these three basic questions, effective teachers also make highly creative decisions. In fact, you will want to consider all of the following variables as you plan instruction.

KNOWLEDGE OF STUDENTS

Effective teachers know their students and what their students need to be successful. You will need to consider and design instruction that will also meet the needs and interests of your students. Additionally, effective teachers understand their students' skills and abilities, and use this knowledge to create learning opportunities.

KNOWLEDGE OF CONTENT

Effective teachers know the content they teach. Hence, you will need to use school district curriculum guides, but also utilize national and state curriculum standards in designing instruction.

KNOWLEDGE OF MATERIALS

Effective teachers use a wide variety of materials to teach their students the content to be learned. They know that nearly all students do better if they can be exposed to content in a variety of ways. For example, you will want to use technology, software, audio-visuals, community resources, equipment, manipulatives, library resources, local guest speakers, and volunteers.

KNOWLEDGE OF LESSON PRESENTATION

Effective teachers use variety in lesson planning and structure based on attributes of the content to be taught and the needs of their learners. For instance, you will want to become familiar with direct instruction, inquiry learning, and thematic instruction.

KNOWLEDGE OF INSTRUCTIONAL STRATEGIES

Effective teachers have a wide range of teaching strategies, and know that determining which method is "right" for a particular lesson depends on many things. Among them are age and developmental level of their students; what the students already know; what they need to know to succeed with the lesson; the subject-matter content; the objective of the lesson; the available people, time, space, and material resources; and the physical setting.

KNOWLEDGE OF STUDENT ASSESSMENT

Effective teachers use student assessment to guide their understanding of student learning and their own classroom teaching. You know that how a student performs is a good reflection of the instruction you provided; therefore, you will want to develop many strategies to informally assess students' progress throughout the lesson.

Sustained Silent Planning Time

Many teachers report feeling rushed for time, and often cut short planning time. However, successful teachers focus on lesson planning. They know that good planning promotes learning, which, in turn, foster better classroom behavior.

It is often more productive to develop your lesson plans in the classroom, since all your materials and resources are close at hand. Therefore, some teachers plan to stay at school at least one day a week until their planning is completed. Other teachers find it useful to come in one day over the weekend while they are fresh and relaxed. However you plan, it is essential that you begin the week fully prepared to teach.

Long-Term Curriculum Mapping, Monthly Overviews, Weekly Overviews, and Daily Plans

Knowing what lies ahead gives you an opportunity to see how you can make all the curricular pieces fit together, smoothly. Your lesson plan book serves as an outline/overview for the instructional events that will occur in your classroom. In order to meet your instructional goals, it is important to set aside designated time for long-term curricular mapping and for drafting monthly overviews, as well as generating weekly and daily lesson plans.

The chart on the next page provides an example of a typical weekly overview. Weekly plans help you transition from the yearly overview and the month long-term plans to daily plans. The week-at-a-glance provides a guide for development of daily detailed lesson plans. The actual lesson plan needs to be more fully developed as you begin your teaching career so you have a clear blueprint for instruction.

As you plan lessons, you will need to consider the best format for the content to be taught. There are different types of lesson structures. For example, you may wish to use the Direct Instruction Lesson Plan when you teach foundational information. For ongoing learning and exploration, you may want to use the Five E's Lesson Plan, a lesson structure suited to the inquiry nature of learning science. Likewise, you may also wish to include thematic curriculum integration. Included on the following page is a rubric resource for use as a guide in lesson planning and in assessing a lesson plan.

view POINT

Frequently, teachers' days are extremely tiring, both physically and mentally. Therefore, experienced teachers recommend that you arrange some planning time on the weekend, if necessary, rather than staying late at school each day.

Time Frame	Monday	Tuesday	Wednesday	Thursday	Friday
Before school					
Lunch					
After school					

For the Week of:

RUBRIC FOR ASSESSING LESSON PLANS

Name _____   Date _____

Subject _____   Lesson _____

1. Specifies desired learner outcomes for lessons	2. Specifies teaching procedures for lessons	3. Specifies resources for lessons
❑ Desired learner outcome(s) described in clear/consistent terms. ❑ Logically sequenced. ❑ Appropriate to student achievement level(s). ❑ Directly linked to unit goals and to state/district/school standards.	❑ Referenced to the objective(s)/outcome. ❑ Appropriate to accomplishing objective(s)/outcome. ❑ Logically sequenced. ❑ Transitions are planned from one activity to another.	❑ Relevance to learning activity. ❑ Lesson plans include specific description of resources, such as title, page, equipment. ❑ Concrete or manipulative materials identified when appropriate. ❑ Creative use of resources.
Comments:	Comments:	Comments:

4. Specifies procedures for assessing student progress	5. Plans for student diversity, abilities and styles	6. Plans address all levels of knowledge and understanding
❑ Written lesson plans include informal assessments of student learning. ❑ Tests and other formal assessments focus directly on instructional goals and objectives and assess only the content that was taught. ❑ Develops and maintains an accurate record of student performance, e.g. grade book anecdotal notes, test scores, portfolio. ❑ Considers multiple sources of assessment data when making instructional decisions.	❑ Presents instruction based on assessment of student's performance. ❑ Provides remedial or enrichment materials/ instruction when appropriate. ❑ Plans individual student conferences to discuss learning or motivational problems. ❑ Varies instructional strategies in accordance with student needs.	❑ Plans require students to memorize important vs. trivial information and to comprehend or interpret information as appropriate. ❑ Plans require students to apply information to real life settings. ❑ Plans require students to identify/clarify complex ideas or to synthesize knowledge by integrating information. ❑ Plans stress depth as well as breadth of content coverage.
Comments:	Comments:	Comments:

DIRECT INSTRUCTION LESSON PLAN

The direct instruction (or direct presentation) lesson plan is best used when introducing new information and when covering a great deal of information. The next page provides a structure for this format.

■ © 2008 Jupiter Images Corporation.

view POINT

Consider using a software program designed for teachers. These generally include several formats for weekly and daily lesson plans. Find a form that suits your unique needs.

DIRECT INSTRUCTION LESSON PLAN

Subject _____   Class/Period_____

Lesson Title _____   Date _____

Time	Lesson Components	Resources
	Lesson Objective (Learner outcomes) ■ What do you want the students to learn? ■ What do you want the students to demonstrate? State Standard: District Outcome:	■ What resources/ materials/ equipment will you use to teach the content? ■ What preparations are necessary?
	Introduction (Focus, anticipatory set, motivation) ■ How will you gain the students' attention? ■ How will you connect students' prior knowledge to new learning? ■ How will you motivate students?	
	Instruction (Content, processes, engagement, differentiation) ■ What strategies will you use to teach the content? ■ How will you sequence the delivery and learning of the content? ■ How will students be actively engaged? ■ How will you differentiate to accommodate all learners?	
	Assessment (Check for understanding, assess learning, assignments for independent skill development) ■ How will you determine the students' level of understanding? ■ How will you document the students' learning?	
	Closure (Summary of learning and preview of subsequent objectives) ■ How will you help students retain information learned? ■ How will you help students apply knowledge learned?	

Form adapted from Kortman and Honaker, 2005

Sample Direct Instruction Lesson Plan

Subject Language Arts

Class/Period 10:40-11:30

Lesson Title Newspaper-Lead Paragraph

Date March 1st

Time	Lesson Components	Resources
10:40 – 10:45	**Lesson Objective** (Learner outcomes) • Explain that the lead paragraph of a news story usually answers who, what, when, where, why, and how. • Determine from selected newspaper articles the information that answers who, what, when, where, why and how. State Standard: L.A.-5.6 District Outcome: Language-5.5	
10:45 – 10:50	**Introduction** (Focus, anticipatory set, motivation) In yesterday's class we learned that the headlines of newspapers are designed to help you read the paper. You all were very good at reading headlines and predicting what the article would be about. Now we're going to learn another way to get the news quickly and easily. The first paragraph of an article is called the lead paragraph; it is designed to help you read the paper and quickly learn all about the outcome of the state basketball tournaments or the latest on state or national events.	
10:50 – 11:10	**Instruction** (Content, processes, engagement, differentiation) • Write who, what, when, where, why, and how in a vertical column on the board (modeling). Ask students to write these words in their notes (active participation). Tell them they will need to use these words in the activity they are about to begin. Tell students that with the help of their partner they will be asked to find information in a newspaper article and write it in a column to the right of their "who, what, when, where, why, how" column. Demonstrate on board where information is to be written. • Walk around room. Ensure students list the information in their notes (check for understanding). Students are more likely to stay on task if teacher is in close proximity. • Ask students to listen carefully as the teacher reads a lead paragraph from a selected article. Ask the class to listen for who the article is about, what happened, when it happened, where it happened, why it happened and how it happened. As students hear the answer to each question, they should write the answer in the designated column of their notes (guided practice). • When the class is finished writing their answers, ask them to share the answers to the following questions: who, what, when, where, why, and how. If all/most students appear to say the correct answers, move on to the next activity.	Sample article with appropriate lead paragraph-- for guided practice.
11:10 – 11:20	**Assessment** (Check for understanding, assess learning, assignments for independent skill development) • Have students work in pairs. Hand out selected news stories, one per student. • Explain that students are to take turns reading the first paragraph out loud to their partners. Then, with the partner's help, each student is to identify the who, what, when, where, why, and how information from the article. • Ask students, "In which paragraph did you find this information?" • Tell students to write the information in the appropriate column in their notes. • Partners are to check for accuracy of the information recorded.	Sample articles with appropriate lead paragraphs--one per student.
11:20 – 11:30	**Closure** (Summary of learning and preview of subsequent objectives) • Observe students' responses. Ensure the tasks are being completed correctly (Check for understanding). When each pair has finished, challenge students to pull information together by asking them to remember, without looking at their notes, all six questions usually answered in the lead paragraph of an article. • Ask students to remember in which paragraph they found the information. • After a brief wait ask students to share questions with their partner and the name of the paragraph where the answers were found.	

Form adapted from Kortman and Honaker, 2005; sample lesson adapted from Enz, Hurwitz and Carlie, 2005.

FIVE E'S LESSON FORMAT

The Five E's (Engagement, Exploration, Explanation, Extension, and Evaluation) is designed for inquiry-driven lessons and is often used for teaching science. The following format provides an example of how this lesson is constructed. An example of this type of lesson may be found on page 119.

Five E's Lesson Outline

Five E's	Possible Activities
Engagement: The activities in this section capture the students' attention, stimulate their thinking, and help them access prior knowledge.	■ Demonstration • teacher and/or student ■ Reading from: • current media release • science journal or book • piece of literature (biography, essay, poem, etc.) ■ Free write ■ Analyze a graphic organizer
Exploration: In this section students are given time to think, plan, investigate, and organize collected information.	■ Reading authentic resources to collect information to: • answer open-ended questions • make a decision ■ Solve a problem ■ Construct a model ■ Experiment design and/or perform
Explanation: Students are now involved in an analysis of their exploration. Their understanding is clarified and modified because of reflective activities.	■ Student analysis and explanation ■ Supporting ideas with evidence ■ Reading and discussion
Extension: This section gives students the opportunity to expand and solidify their understanding of the concept and/or apply it to a real-world situation.	■ Problem-solving ■ Experimental inquiry ■ Thinking skills activities ■ Classifying, abstracting, error analysis ■ Decision-making
Evaluation: By the end of the lesson there should be a means of determining how well students have learned, and can apply, the new concepts and the related vocabulary. Such evaluation does not have to be at the end of the lesson. It can be embedded in other phases.	■ Teacher- and/or student-generated scoring tools or rubrics

Adapted from Bybee, et. al, 2006

5 E'S LESSON PLAN

Subject _____	Class/Period _____
Lesson Title _____	Date _____

Lesson Objective

State Standard: District Outcome:

Engagement

Exploration

Explanation

Extension

Evaluation

Form adapted from Bybee, et. al, 2006

Curriculum Integration

Thematic instruction is an exciting way that effective teachers help students learn. The following special feature describes how Mrs. Lopez begins to develop an integrated, thematic unit on the Way West. She identifies the interests of her students, and works with district and state curriculum guidelines to develop her unit.

KWL

To determine topics of interest, Mrs. Lopez uses the KWL strategy. The KWL chart below presents the initial outcome of these efforts. KWL stands for "What We **K**now, What We **W**ant to Learn, and What We **L**earned." Prior to the unit, students complete the Know and Want columns. As a closure, students can then fill in the final column and analyze questions previously asked.

Sample KWL

What We Know About	What We Want to Learn	What We Learned
■ Gold Rush in 1849 ■ Wagon trains ■ Free land ■ Many people died	■ Who were the people who left their homes? ■ How long did wagon trips take? ■ Why did the Indians attack the wagon trains? ■ How did the people survive this trip?	■ Irish people were one of the largest groups because of the Potato Famine. ■ The people survived the trip because their families were strong, they planned well, and they rationed their food.

Utilizing the information attained, Mrs. Lopez developed a curriculum plan. This process allowed her to consider district and state requirements, and merge them with the students' interests and prior knowledge.

TOPIC WEB

A topic web is used as a planning strategy to:

■ See natural linkages between topics in the curriculum;

■ Consider the range of resources that could be used;

■ Develop a tentative timeline.

view POINT

At the end of the instructional time, ask students to summarize what they have learned. Have students record in the "What We Learned" column on their KWL chart.

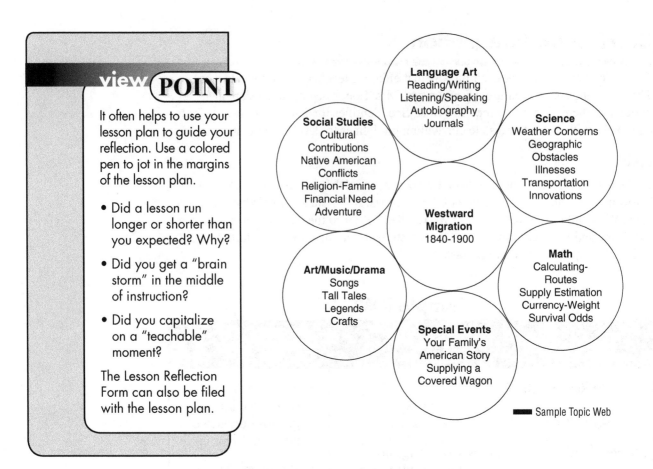

Language Art
Reading/Writing
Listening/Speaking
Autobiography
Journals

Social Studies
Cultural
Contributions
Native American
Conflicts
Religion-Famine
Financial Need
Adventure

Science
Weather Concerns
Geographic
Obstacles
Illnesses
Transportation
Innovations

Westward Migration
1840-1900

Art/Music/Drama
Songs
Tall Tales
Legends
Crafts

Math
Calculating-
Routes
Supply Estimation
Currency-Weight
Survival Odds

Special Events
Your Family's
American Story
Supplying a
Covered Wagon

▬ Sample Topic Web

After developing a topic web with your students, use the information to guide your planning. You may be able to design multiple lessons incorporating the topic web. The following chart provides one example.

Sample Lesson Planning Guide

Subject →	Topic →	Objective →	Activities
Social Studies	Cultural Contributions	To identify the cultural contributions of the Irish community	Learn Irish ballads Analyze text of ballads for contributions

Time for Reflection

Time is one of a teacher's most valuable commodities. To make the best use of your time, set aside 10–15 minutes at the end of each day for reflection. Think about all of the events that went well and why; then think about what you would change about the day to enhance student learning. These ideas and insights build thoughtful teaching practice. The Curriculum Lesson Reflection Form is a more formalized way to assess your instruction and planning.

CURRICULUM LESSON REFLECTION FORM

Date _____   Grade _____

Subject _____   Hour _____

To Celebrate!! (Identify one positive element to include next time.)

To Grow On!! (Identify one element to improve next time.)

To Implement!! (How will you implement area to improve?)

Research suggests that, as effective teachers plan the content of their lessons, they simultaneously plan for student management. They consider how they will transition students from one activity to another. They consider how they will distribute and collect materials. While experienced teachers plan this intuitively, most new teachers do not immediately consider these critical components of instruction (Enz, Hurwitz and Carlile, 2007).

Hence, teacher educators recommend that teachers include management strategies as part of their lesson plans. This reminder keeps these important aspects of managing instruction in the forefront of their thinking.

Enz, B., Hurwitz, S, and Carlile, B. (2007). *Coaching the student teacher: A developmental approach* (3rd ed.). Kendall/Hunt Publishing Company. Dubuque, IA.

evaluation QUESTIONS ?

- How do you organize lesson planning for effective instruction?
- How will you incorporate curriculum integration?

Questions for Reflection

INSTRUCTIONAL PLANNING

- How do you plan to incorporate state standards when planning for the grade level/content area you wish to teach?
- How will you developed long-term curriculum plans that reflect all the instructional units you are required to teach during the course of the year?
- How will you write an effective lesson objective?
- How will you use the direct instruction plan?
- How will you use the Five E's lesson plan?
- How will you integrate curriculum units?
- How will you consider transitions, distribution of materials in your lessons?

CURRICULUM INTEGRATION

- How will you use a KWL chart or topic web to design instruction to meet student interests?
- How will you integrate multiple content areas into a lesson?

Instruction

> **"**Tell me, and I'll listen. Show me, and I'll understand. Involve me, and I'll learn.**"**
>
> —TETON LAKOTA INDIAN

Student Engagement

How a teacher begins his or her lesson, how he or she captures the students' interest and sustains student attention, is critical to student learning and achievement. All of these activities fall under the heading of active student engagement. Studies reveal that students who actively participate in a lesson tend to be more accountable, responsible, and successful than students who are merely bystanders. Research also suggests that students who are actively engaged retain more information. Students remember:

- 10% of what they read
- 20% of what they hear
- 30% of what they see
- 50% of what they see and hear
- 70% of what they say
- 90% of what they say while doing

> **Mentor Voices**
>
> ➤ "Planning is the first step to good classroom management."

EFFECTIVE INSTRUCTIONAL STRATEGIES

Three instructional strategies have emerged from the literature as being particularly effective when teaching learners with diverse learning characteristics: peer and cross-age tutoring, cooperative learning and flexible grouping.

Peer/Cross-age Tutoring Peer and cross-age tutoring operates on the principle that one-on-one instruction will increase students' performance in academic areas and improve students' social skills and behavior more than whole- or small-group instruction. Cross-age tutoring usually involves older students tutoring younger students, while peer-tutoring involves same age students working together. Both students benefit academically and socially from the learning experience. Both also become winners when a student with a learning disability tutors a younger student. The exceptional student wins a wealth of self-esteem.

Cooperative Learning Cooperative learning strategies operate on the age-old principle of social psychology that people working together toward a common goal can achieve more than individuals working separately. Cooperative learning strategies are characterized by a heterogeneous group of students working together, typically in groups of two to six, on lessons assigned by the teacher. They are tested individually, but are rewarded based on the accomplishments of the group as a whole. Cooperative learning has been well documented in research literature as not only improving achievement, but also improving social skills of mixed-ability students, including exceptional students.

Flexible Grouping Students can be grouped in a number of ways including by interests, skills to be learned, subject proficiency, level of basic skills, and prior knowledge. The present trend in general education is toward heterogeneous or mixed-ability grouping, in which students with a wide range of achievement levels are put together for instruction. Since students with different exceptionalities are spending more and more of their school day in general education, they benefit academically and socially from mixed-ability grouping.

Providing opportunities for students to work in groups to discuss and document their learning is essential for retention of new information. It is important to building classroom community that you deliberately vary group sizes and objectives. The following suggestions provide ways to "mix-it-up" in a heterogeneous manner.

- *Deck of Cards or UNO Cards*—Randomly pass out cards. You may have the students meet with people of the same number, the same color, or the same suit.

- *Famous Pairs*—For partner activities, make a set of index cards with famous pairs on them. Pass them out to the students and have them find their match. You can use names like Bert and Ernie, Fred and Wilma, Curious George and the Man with the Yellow Hat, Robinson Crusoe and Friday, etc. Update those who may become out of date each year and add popular ones to it.

- *Paint Samples*—Go to a hardware store where you can get paint samples in clusters of 3 or 4 complimenting colors. Cut apart the colors and have students select one paint chip/color upon entering class. Then, have students find their like color group for their small group assignments.

- *Count Off*—Using the ever-favorite "count off" strategy, ask all the "ones" to form a group, all the "twos" form a group, etc.

- *Student Choice*—Allow students to group themselves based on topics of interest.

Case Study

Let's review the following lesson plan that Mr. Block developed for his first grade students. As you read his lesson, consider how he used grouping strategies and active learning to keep his active primary students engaged in the learning process.

Did you notice that a majority of the lesson included student activity? Mr. Block's lesson about camouflage could have ended with the reading of the book. However, the retention of only this information may have been greatly limited. Mr. Block's hands-on lesson enabled all students to actively process this information. Let's consider how much they may have learned by using our retention chart. As a reminder, students remember:

- 10% of what they read
- 20% of what they hear
- 30% of what they see
- 50% of what they see and hear
- 70% of what they say
- 90% of what they say while doing

Sample 5 E's Lesson Plan

Subject _Science_	Class/Period _1:45–2:30_
	Date _February 21st_
Lesson Title _Camouflage: Eating All the Little Fishes_	

Lesson Objective
The first graders will learn how camouflage helps animals survive.

State Standard: _Science: Grade 1.4_   District Outcome: _Science: Grade 1 Prediction_

Engagement
Mr. Block reads the story *How to Hide a Butterfly and Other Insects* by Ruth Heller. This simple text has color pictures that demonstrate how insects use camouflage to hide from their enemies and prey. The first graders enjoy looking for the hidden insects.

Exploration
Using the Uno cards, Mr. Block organizes the students into six groups of four students each. He gives them the following instructions.

- Each group has a different colored, patterned cloth that is placed on the table, and each table has a tiny cup containing many different colored paper fish.
- Mr. Block asks for one student in each group to sprinkle the fish onto the cloth.
- Mr. Block turns out the lights and allows the students a minute to adjust their eyes.
- The students are given 20 seconds to find as many of the fish as they can and remove them from the cloth.
- Mr. Block turns the light back on and tells the students to freeze.

The fish left on the cloth are sorted and counted by color.

Explanation
Mr. Block asks the students if they notice anything about the fish that were left on the cloth. The students in each group should realize that the fish left were the same color as the cloth.

Extension
Mr. Block asks the students to think about, then write, their explanation of how the fish in their experiment are like the butterflies and insects in the story, *How to Hide a Butterfly and Other Insects*. Mr. Block gives each group chart paper and markers to record their thoughts.

Evaluation
Mr. Block gives each student drawing paper and crayons. He asks the students to draw a habitat (a concept previously learned), and to draw pictures of camouflaged animals that might live in this habitat. As the students complete this task, Mr. Block circulates and asks students about their unique creations.

Form adapted from Bybee, et. al, 2006; Sample lesson adapted from Enz, Bergeron and Wolfe, 2006

TEACHER BEHAVIORS LEADING TO STUDENT SUCCESS

Keeping students engaged also means that the teacher is prepared. The following list offers ideas for initiating your success.

What to Do	How to Do It
Set clear expectations.	Have 2 or 3 guidelines for behavior.
Provide engaging lessons that encourage active participation.	Use games, activity cards, and whiteboards for multiple responses.
Utilize effective organization skills.	Be prepared with all paperwork before class time.
Establish and maintain routines.	Have students fulfill job responsibilities.
Effectively focus and retain student and group attention.	Use multiple strategies. Have a good set. Have relevant activities. Adjust to age-appropriate attention span.
Provide clear instruction.	Plan. Plan. Plan.
Build positive relationships.	Relate to students in their areas of interest.
Provide relevant learning choices.	Focus on process of learning, not just product.
Understand and adapt to student needs.	Use a variety of learning strategies.

SELF-ASSESSMENT OR OBSERVATION PROTOCOL

Teacher Name _____ Subject _____

Date _____ ❑ Self-Assessment ❑ Observation

Instruction Criteria	Rating		
	Low		High
Teacher stimulates interest in lesson by actively involving students or by asking thought-provoking questions.	1	2	3
Teacher connects new learning with something familiar.	1	2	3
Teacher provides appropriate concrete visual models.	1	2	3
Teacher provides opportunities for overt participation, such as simultaneous note-taking and small-group activities.	1	2	3
Teacher presents information in a logical sequence, going from the simplest to more difficult concepts.	1	2	3
Teacher models appropriate responses using visual display.	1	2	3
Teacher provides critical information on board, screen, or chart.	1	2	3
Teacher checks student understanding and responses throughout lesson.	1	2	3
Comments:			

Teacher Responses to Common Student Learning Needs Effective teachers know their students and what their students need to be successful. These teachers also have a wide range of teaching strategies to use when students are having difficulty. The following strategies are useful for students who might be experiencing these common concerns.

Drawing Conclusions and Making Inferences

- Teaching thinking skills directly
- Draw a parallel to a situation the student might have prior experience with

Working in Groups

- Provide a partner
- Provide student with a task or position of leadership
- Provide more structure by defining tasks and listing steps

Remembering

- Provide a checklist
- Provide cues
- Have students make notes to self
- Teach memory skills
- Teach use of acronyms
- Teach use of mnemonic devices

Understanding Cause/Effect; Anticipating Consequences

- Use concrete examples
- Use real-life situations
- Directly teach cause/effect
- Brainstorming
- Role playing
- Simulation activities

Spelling

- Dictate word; ask student to repeat it
- Avoid traditional spelling lists
- Teach short, easy words in context
- Have students make flash cards
- Hang words from ceiling, or post on walls for constant visual cues
- Provide a tactile aid to spelling (sandpaper letters, saltbox, etc.)

Getting Started

- Give work in smaller amounts
- Provide immediate feedback
- Sequence work

- Provide time parameters
- Check on progress
- Peer tutor
- Give cue to begin work

Expressing in Writing

- Accept alternate forms of reporting:
  - oral report
  - taped interview
  - maps
  - photographic essay
  - panel discussion
- Student dictates work to others
- Have student prepare only notes or outline on subject
- Shorten amount required

Understanding What Is Read

- Reduce the language level
- Become more concrete
- Reduce amount of new ideas
- Provide experiences for a frame of reference
- Provide study guide
- Give organizational help
- Provide alternate media
- Use fill-in-the-blank technique

Learning by Listening

- Provide visuals
- Use flash cards
- Have student close eyes and visualize the information
- Teach use of acronyms
- Give explanations in small distinct steps
- Provide study guide

Paying Attention to Print

- Select a text at independent level
- Highlight cues
- Underline, number
- Keep desk free of extra materials

© PhotoCreate 2008. Used under license from Shutterstock, Inc.

Reading Textbooks

- Use lower level or adaptive text
- Tape text
- Shorten amount of required reading
- Have students read aloud in small groups
- Allow extra time for reading
- Reduce reading requirements
- Put main ideas on index cards
- Use a buddy or a work group
- Pre-teach vocabulary

Supporting Self-Expression

- Accept alternative forms of reporting:
  - written report
  - artwork or exhibit
  - chart/graph
  - bulletin board
  - photos
- Ask questions requiring short answers
- Provide prompts
- Give rules for class discussion
- Let student speak in smaller groups
- Allow taped reports

Differentiation

Your students will be very diverse. Some will speak English, some will be learning to speak English and some may speak through sign language or some other communication device. In the classroom, students will run, walk, and roll in wheelchairs. Just as they communicate and move in different ways, your students will also learn in different ways.

Your regular lesson plans and instructional units can be given added depth by incorporating the curriculum and instructional modifications you have identified for your students with exceptionalities.

DIFFERENTIATING FOR STUDENTS IN SPECIAL EDUCATION

Special education teachers in your school will help provide the support for *all* students to be successful in your classroom, the school, and the larger community. In order to receive special support for students in your classroom, they must be identified as having an exceptionality. Identification procedures and special education services are governed by specific federal and state legislation.

This section addresses some of the questions teachers typically have about teaching students who are receiving special education services. The information in this section is illustrated through Mark, an elementary student who has exceptional learning needs. The use of this case study is in no way prescriptive, but merely an example of how the concepts and ideas in this chapter are applicable in a variety of school settings and with different instructional approaches. The goal remains the same: to create inclusive learning communities in which all students are valued.

Case Study 📄 Mark

Mark Barger is a seven-year-old student in second grade at Apple Elementary School. Mark is a socially active student who has quite a few friends, likes school, and enjoys participation in many extracurricular activities such as scouts and baseball. Because of his gregarious personality, Mark has always been well liked by students, teachers, and staff.

Mark's mother reported that his medical history was normal at birth. She reported that Mark had severe pneumonia when he was two, but felt there were no negative effects from his illness. In addition, Mrs. Barger reported that Mark seemed very normal as a baby and toddler (e.g., sitting up, crawling, walking) when compared to her other children.

Teachers first noticed Mark's learning delays when he was in preschool. Although minor at the time, his inattention and hyperactive behaviors eventually became more prominent as the academic demands increased and his teachers required him to attend to activities for longer periods of time. Despite his academic and behavioral problems, Mark's friendly smile and teacher-pleasing behaviors always seemed to prevent his teachers from giving him poor grades and reporting his minor incidents of misconduct. Often when Mark became too frustrated, he would daydream or sketch.

Finally, at the age of seven, Mark's second grade teacher, Mrs. Smith, who had known Mark for some time, initiated a referral. She was surprised that teachers had not referred him earlier. Mrs. Smith referred him for special services because she had observed Mark's inability to read. She also noticed that Mark had a short attention span and was hyperactive. Mark could not remember letters or simple words from one day to the next. He reversed several letters. Although his handwriting was legible when copying, he was unable to write or spell a given letter or simple word. Mark was diagnosed as having learning disabilities specifically in reading, writing, and spelling.

Mrs. Barger felt that all of the pieces to the puzzle were beginning to fit into place. She was relieved to learn that Mark qualified to receive special services earlier that year.

Although she still did not agree with the label of "learning disabled," she was happy to see him finally get some help. He was in a regular second-grade classroom. His special education teacher, Mr. Roland, visited him daily in his class to work on reading skills. Mrs. Smith spent extra time with him before and after school, providing him with extra practice opportunities on skills. Peer and cross-aged tutors also provided short lessons with Mark.

Besides drawing, Mark demonstrated above-average intelligence in mathematics. He often solved his fifth grade sister's math problems after she read the story problems aloud. Mark's father reported that he could solve complex puzzles and games (checkers, chess, trivia, etc.) quicker than his older brother and sister.

A Brief Overview of Special Education

What Is Special Education? The Education for all Handicapped Students Act was passed in 1975, amended in 1986 and 1992, and re-authorized as the Individuals with Disabilities Education Act (IDEA) in 1991, 1997, and 2004. It established the right to a free and appropriate public education (FAPE) in the least restrictive environment (LRE) for students with exceptionalities. The law mandates that each student receiving special educational services have an Individual Education Program (IEP). The IEP is a written document developed by a multidisciplinary team, which includes the student, the student's parents (guardian), the student's regular and special education teachers, and other school administrative and support personnel. It describes the student's current level of functioning, their goals and objectives, the types of support the student needs, and the dates for the initiation and duration of that support. Students may need intermittent or sustained support services. These supports may be limited to particular environments or pervade all aspects of the student's life. Examples of the educational supports provided for Mark will be described later in this section.

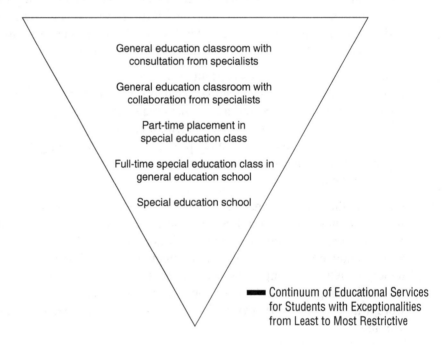

General education classroom with
consultation from specialists

General education classroom with
collaboration from specialists

Part-time placement in
special education class

Full-time special education class in
general education school

Special education school

▬ Continuum of Educational Services
for Students with Exceptionalities
from Least to Most Restrictive

Where Does Special Education Happen? Educational placements for students with special needs range from the most restrictive, hospitalization, to the least restrictive, the regular classroom. Special education supports are sometimes delivered in a specific place, either removed from the regular classroom or within the classroom. However, special education is not a place; rather, it is the range of supports designed to meet the needs of students challenged with special learning needs. Several trends have been witnessed in special education:

■ Classrooms and schools have become more inclusive and less segregated.

   Example: Students with physical exceptionalities are included in general education.

- Curriculum has focused more on higher-level outcomes and problem-solving in naturally occurring situations, and less on remediation.

  Example: Students with exceptionalities are included instructionally in general education.

- Classrooms have evolved into caring communities of diverse learners.

  Example: Students with exceptionalities are included socially in general education.

- Regular education teachers, special education teachers, parents, and school staff work together as problem-solving teams.

  Example: Collaboration is a critical component empowering educators to maintain inclusive educational environments for all students.

The trend toward including all students in regular classrooms with the special education supports they need to be successful has been called the *Inclusion Movement*. Regular education classrooms in which general and special educators work together to meet all students' physical, instructional and social needs at least 80 percent of their school day are considered inclusive classrooms.

Applied Case Study

Mark spends his day in a regular second-grade classroom. His teacher collaborates and co-teaches with the special education teacher during Language Arts.

What Are the Different Types of Exceptionalities? There are 12 categories of exceptionality identified by the federal government. These categories and their names may vary somewhat from state to state:

- Mental retardation
- Specific learning disabilities
- Serious emotional disturbances
- Speech or language impairments
- Hearing impairments
- Visual impairments
- Deaf blindness
- Orthopedic impairments
- Multiple disabilities
- Autism
- Traumatic brain injury
- Other health problems

States also offer special educational supports for students identified as gifted and talented, and students having academic difficulty who may be labeled "at risk." You must remember, however, that categorical labels have limited instructional value, serving primarily as a means for allocating federal funds to pay for special education services. The U.S. Department of Education developed definitions for each of these categories, and each state has developed different rules and regulations specifying implementation procedures to comply with the Individuals with Disabilities Education Act.

What Causes Exceptionalities? Usually there are several interrelated variables that may result in an individual having an exceptionality. Contributing factors may include heredity, environment, or a combination of the two. General causes of some exceptionalities are:

- Genetic (e.g., Down syndrome).
- Metabolic (e.g., phenylketonuria or PKU).
- Environmental factors (e.g., lead poisoning, fetal alcohol syndrome).
- Chronic illness (e.g., asthma, diabetes, HIV, cystic fibrosis).
- Brain injury (e.g., asphyxia).
- Accidents (e.g., spinal cord injuries).
- Congenital birth defects (e.g., spina bifida, cerebral palsy).

The important task for the teacher is to focus on providing the necessary support for students to be successful in the classroom, rather than trying to determine the exact cause of an exceptionality.

How Do the Referral Processes Work? Before you make a formal referral to someone in your special education department about a student who may be a candidate for special services, check your district and state guidelines. According to most guidelines, you are required to do the following:

1. Experiment using a few *procedural or instructional modifications.*
2. Consult with other professionals. Many elementary schools have *pre-referral assistance teams (PAT),* which commonly comprise four or five professionals: other classroom teachers, a special or remedial educator, a counselor, a principal or vice-principal, and perhaps a communication disorders specialist. One or more of the PAT members might observe your student in your classroom and collaborate with you to develop alternative strategies.
3. Initiate a *formal referral* through special education.

What Is the Formal Referral and Identification Process for Special Education? A referral for a special education evaluation can be initiated by a classroom teacher, by other school personnel, or by a parent. Assessments are conducted by a special education *multidisciplinary team (MDT).* For example, Mark's MDT team included a regular second-grade teacher, a special education teacher, and a school psychologist. This team may also include a communication disorders specialist, a counselor, a behavioral interventionist, among other professionals. Approved instruments and procedures are used to evaluate the referred student's current levels of functioning in the following areas:

- *Instructional* (general intelligence, academic performance, communication).
- *Physical* (motor abilities, health, vision, and hearing).
- *Social* (social-emotional functioning).

After the assessment results are collected, the team shares the results of the assessments with the parents. In collaboration with the parents and the classroom teacher, the team determines whether the student in question qualifies for special education services according to federal and state guidelines. To be eligible to receive special education services, a student must meet the eligibility criteria for at least one of the categories (e.g., specific learning disabilities, as in the case of Mark).

What Is an Individualized Education Program (IEP)? Individualized Education Programs are mandated by law for each student who is receiving special education services. Part of Mark's IEP is on the following page. The IEP provides a written document that describes the following sections:

1. Present educational level and planned goals and objectives
2. Type and location of support services
3. The extent to which the student will be in regular classroom or other natural environments with students without exceptionalities
4. Date for initiation and duration of special education services
5. Procedures to evaluate student's progress
6. Description of Least Restrictive Environment
7. Transition services

> ## Mentor Voices
>
> ➤ "Learning strategies to work with special needs students or students learning a second language actually helps you to be a better teacher."

© 2008 Jupiter Images Corporation.

Sample IEP Snapshot

Date of IEP Meeting: 10-5	Anticipated Duration of IEP October **to** October	IEP Type: ☐ Initial ☒ Annual ☐ Interim

Student: Mark Barger School: Apple Elementary Grade: 2 Current Placement: Regular Class/ Sp Ed Consultant/Co-teacher Birthdate: July 17	District Representative: Dr. Ryan, Principal Regular Education Teacher: Mrs. Smith, 2nd Grade Special Education Teacher: Mr. Roland Parent(s): Rene & Bob Barger Evaluator: Dr. Duffy, Psychologist Student: Mark Barger

Present Educational Level	Annual Goal	Instructional Objectives	Evaluation
Language Arts: Strengths 1. Can successfully retell short stories in sequence, often elaborating, creating additional details. 2. Writes legibly when copying manuscript. 3. Talented artist. Weaknesses 1. Frequently unable to recall names or sounds of letters, letter combinations and words. 2. Reverses and inverts letters. 3. Unable to spell one-syllable words. 4. Does not complete assignments.	Mark will demonstrate improvement in Language Arts Skills by 4-6 months.	1. When presented with letters (consonants/ short and long vowel combinations), Mark will say name and sounds correctly, 40-60/minute. 2. When dictated sounds (consonants/short and long vowel combinations), words or phonetically controlled sentences, Mark will write (spell) the letter/s, words or sentences correctly 40-60 letters/minute and 15 words/minute. 3. When presented with phonetic-controlled words, Mark will sound out blended words at a rate of 80-100 words/minute with 90% accuracy. 4. When presented with phonetic-controlled stories, Mark will read 200 words/minute. 5. Mark will dictate original stories incorporating words with lesson's sounds with a minimum of 5 sentences.	Daily charting. Teacher and Mark self-monitor ↓ Journal and Portfolio

What Roles Do Teachers, Students, and Parents Play in the Development and Implementation of IEPs? Both the general education teacher and the special education teacher should actively participate in writing and implementing the student's plan. Parents must be invited to the IEP meeting. The team should attempt to accommodate the parents' schedule when holding these meetings. It is vital that the parents participate in designing every component of the document. They should understand the process, including the transition plans between elementary and high school, high school and college, and high school and work. Parents should also work with support staff and help develop transportation plans. Parents should understand their right to contest or appeal any feature of their student's IEP. When appropriate, the student should also be actively involved in preparing the team plan.

Applied Case Study

Mark participated in his IEP development.

Ideally, you will have been an active participant in the multidisciplinary team IEP meeting when the supports necessary for your student were developed. Time and personnel constraints may have precluded your participation, in which case, consult with your special education staff to obtain:

- A copy of the student's IEP.
- The level of support you will be given to help meet the needs of a student with exceptionalities placed in your classroom.
- Your student's interests and any items or events in which they enjoy participating.
- Academic performance and instructional approaches from which the student has benefited.
- Behavioral approaches that have been successful in promoting responsible self-determination.
- Medications your student may be taking and medical problems that could interfere with his/her education (e.g., seizures, asthma attacks).

Modifications in Curriculum and Instruction Modifying the curriculum content or the instructional strategies in any general education classroom can be accomplished through creative thinking and diligent collaboration between the general educator and the special educators. Effective collaboration can facilitate the purpose of modification: to enable an individual student to compensate for instructional, physical, or social challenges. Modifications allow the student to use existing skill repertoires while promoting the acquisition of new skills and knowledge. Instruction is often modified to allow for partial participation. This implies some level of active involvement in a lesson activity acknowledging that not all students learn the same material in the same way. Some of Mark's curriculum modifications are identified on page 133.

As you view the curriculum and the diversity of the student needs in the classroom, you may sometimes feel overwhelmed about what can be changed. The following modifications, outlined by Ottlinger and Kohlhepp, can be made.

- **Adapt Instructional Strategies**—Vary presentation techniques, pacing, assignments, and test adaptations.

- **Use of Materials and Devices**—Use portable devices or materials that enhance an individual's performance. Items may be commercial or teacher-made. Adaptive devices and communication tools, as well as alternative text materials, fall into this category.

- **Use of Social Supports**—Use any self-management tools to organize instructional activities. Use any type of verbal, physical, supervisory support, peer buddies, tutors, or personal assistants. This assistance may be necessary for long or short timeframes.

- **Adapt the Environment**—Change the actual physical environment; move furniture and obtain smaller chairs, use ramps or other wheelchair-accessible facilities.

Mentor Voices

"Knowing the curriculum and the standards frees you to develop creative lessons."

Sample Curriculum Modification Checklist

Check ☒ all modifications that are appropriate and necessary for this student.

Student _Mark Barger_ DOB _7/17_ Date _10/05_

Completed by _Ms. Smith and Mr. Roland_

INSTRUCTIONAL STRATEGIES

Presentation of Subject Matter
- ❑ Teach to student's learning style
  - ❑ Linguistic ❑ Logical/Math ❑ Musical
  - ❑ Spatial ❑ Bodily/Kinesthetic ❑ Interpersonal
  - ❑ Experiential Learning ❑ Multi-sensory
- ☒ Utilize specialized curriculum
- ❑ Teacher tape lectures/discussions for replay
- ❑ Provide notes: teacher or peer copy
- ❑ Functional application of academic skills
- ❑ Present demonstrations (model)
- ❑ Utilize manipulatives
- ❑ Emphasize critical information
- ❑ Pre-teach vocabulary
- ☒ Make/use vocabulary files
- ☒ Reduce language level or reading level of assignment
- ❑ Use total communication
- ❑ Use facilitated communication
- ❑ Share activities
- ❑ Use visual sequences
- Other_____

Pacing
- ❑ Adjust time requirements
- ❑ Vary activity often
- ☒ Allow breaks
- ❑ Omit assignments requiring copy in timed situation
- ❑ School texts sent home for summer preview
- ❑ Home set of texts/materials for preview/review
- Other_____

Assignments
- ❑ Give directions in small, distinct steps:
  - ❑ Rewrite ❑ Use picture ❑ Verbalize
- ❑ Use written back-up for oral directions
- ❑ Lower difficulty level
- ❑ Shorten assignment
- ☒ Reduce paper and pencil tasks
- ☒ Read or tape record directions
- ☒ Use pictorial directions
- ❑ Give extra cues or prompts
- ☒ Allow student to record or type assignment
- ☒ Adapt worksheets, packets
- ❑ Utilize compensatory procedures by providing alternate assignment strategy when demands of class conflict with student capabilities
- ❑ Avoid penalizing for spelling errors
- ❑ Avoid penalizing for penmanship or sloppiness
- Other_____

Testing Adaptations
- ☒ Oral ☒ Taped
- ☒ Use visuals
- ❑ Preview language of test questions
- ❑ Applications in real setting
- ❑ Test administered by resource person
- ❑ Modify format: ❑ short ans ❑ mult choice ❑ essay
  - ❑ discussion ❑ T/F ❑ adjust time ❑ adjust length
- Other_____

SOCIAL SUPPORTS

Self-management/Follow-through
- ☒ Visual daily schedule
- ❑ Calendars
- ❑ Check often for comprehension/review
- ❑ Request parent reinforcement
- ❑ Have student repeat directions
- ❑ Teach study skills
- ❑ Use study sheets to organize material
- ❑ Design/write/use long term assignment timelines
- ❑ Review and practice in real situations
- ❑ Plan for generalizations
- ❑ Teach skill in several settings/environments
- Other_____

Social Interaction Support
- ☒ Personal advocacy
- ☒ Peer tutoring
- ❑ Structure activities to promote social interaction
- ❑ Focus social process instead of activity/end product
- ❑ Structure shared experiences in school/extracurricular
- ☒ Cooperative learning groups
- ☒ Multiple/rotating peers
- ❑ Teach friendship skills/sharing/negotiation
- ❑ Teach social communication skills
- Other_____

Motivation and Reinforcement
- ❑ Verbal
- ❑ Non-verbal
- ❑ Positive reinforcement
- ❑ Concrete reinforcement
- ❑ Plan motivating sequences of activities
- ❑ Reinforce initiation
- ❑ Offer choice
- ❑ Emphasize strengths/interests
- Other _Charting self growth_

ENVIRONMENT
- ❑ Preferential seating
- ❑ Plan Seating
  - ❑ Bus ❑ Classroom ❑ Lunch ❑ Auditorium
- ❑ Alter physical room arrangement
- ❑ Define areas concretely
- ❑ Reduce distractions
  - ❑ Visual ❑ Auditory ❑ Spatial ❑ Motion
- ❑ Teach positive rules for use of space
- ❑ Contracts
- Other _Charting—Self-Growth_

MATERIAL AND DEVICES
- ❑ Arrangement of material on page
- ☒ Taped texts and/or other materials: science and math
- ❑ Highlighted texts/study guides
- ❑ Use supplementary materials
- ❑ Note-taking assistance
- ❑ Type teacher material
- ❑ Large print
- ❑ Special Equipment: ❑ electric typewriter ❑ computer
  - ❑ calculator ❑ phone adaptations ❑ video recorder
- ❑ Community Resources
- Other _Tape recorder, audio card reader_

CURRICULUM MODIFICATION CHECKLIST

Check ☒ all modifications that are appropriate and necessary for this student.

Student _____ DOB _____ Date _____

Completed by _____

INSTRUCTIONAL STRATEGIES

Presentation of Subject Matter
- ❏ Teach to student's learning style
  - ❏ Linguistic ❏ Logical/Math ❏ Musical
  - ❏ Spatial ❏ Bodily/Kinesthetic ❏ Interpersonal
  - ❏ Experiential Learning ❏ Multi-sensory
- ❏ Utilize specialized curriculum
- ❏ Teacher tape lectures/discussions for replay
- ❏ Provide notes: teacher or peer copy
- ❏ Functional application of academic skills
- ❏ Present demonstrations (model)
- ❏ Utilize manipulatives
- ❏ Emphasize critical information
- ❏ Pre-teach vocabulary
- ❏ Make/use vocabulary files
- ❏ Reduce language level of reading level of assignment
- ❏ Use total communication
- ❏ Use facilitated communication
- ❏ Share activities
- ❏ Use visual sequences
- Other_____

Pacing
- ❏ Adjust time requirements
- ❏ Vary activity often
- ❏ Allow breaks
- ❏ Omit assignments requiring copy in timed situation
- ❏ School texts sent home for summer preview
- ❏ Home set of texts/materials for preview/review
- Other_____

Assignments
- ❏ Give directions in small, distinct steps:
  - ❏ Rewrite ❏ Use picture ❏ Verbalize
- ❏ Use written back-up for oral directions
- ❏ Lower difficulty level
- ❏ Shorten assignment
- ❏ Reduce paper and pencil tasks
- ❏ Read or tape record directions
- ❏ Use pictorial directions
- ❏ Give extra cues or prompts
- ❏ Allow student to record or type assignment
- ❏ Adapt worksheets, packets
- ❏ Utilize compensatory procedures by providing alternate assignment strategy when demands of class conflict with student capabilities
- ❏ Avoid penalizing for spelling errors
- ❏ Avoid penalizing for penmanship or sloppiness
- Other_____

Testing Adaptations
- ❏ Oral ❏ Taped
- ❏ Use visuals
- ❏ Preview language of test questions
- ❏ Applications in real setting
- ❏ Test administered by resource person
- ❏ Modify format: ❏ short ans ❏ mult choice ❏ essay
  - ❏ discussion ❏ T/F ❏ adjust time ❏ adjust length
- Other_____

SOCIAL SUPPORTS

Self-management/Follow-through
- ❏ Visual daily schedule
- ❏ Calendars
- ❏ Check often for comprehension/review
- ❏ Request parent reinforcement
- ❏ Have student repeat directions
- ❏ Teach study skills
- ❏ Use study sheets to organize material
- ❏ Design/write/use long term assignment timelines
- ❏ Review and practice in real situations
- ❏ Plan for generalizations
- ❏ Teach skill in several settings/environments
- Other_____

Social Interaction Support
- ❏ Personal advocacy
- ❏ Peer tutoring
- ❏ Structure activities to promote social interaction
- ❏ Focus social process instead of activity/end product
- ❏ Structure shared experiences in school/extracurricular
- ❏ Cooperative learning groups
- ❏ Multiple/rotating peers
- ❏ Teach friendship skills/sharing/negotiation
- ❏ Teach social communication skills
- Other_____

Motivation and Reinforcement
- ❏ Verbal
- ❏ Non-verbal
- ❏ Positive reinforcement
- ❏ Concrete reinforcement
- ❏ Plan motivating sequences of activities
- ❏ Reinforce initiation
- ❏ Offer choice
- ❏ Emphasize strengths/interests
- Other Charting self growth_____

ENVIRONMENT
- ❏ Preferential seating
- ❏ Plan Seating
  - ❏ Bus ❏ Classroom ❏ Lunch ❏ Auditorium
- ❏ Alter physical room arrangement
- ❏ Define areas concretely
- ❏ Reduce distractions
  - ❏ Visual ❏ Auditory ❏ Spatial ❏ Motion
- ❏ Teach positive rules for use of space
- ❏ Contracts
- Other_____

MATERIAL AND DEVICES
- ❏ Arrangement of material on page
- ❏ Taped texts and/or other materials: science and math
- ❏ Highlighted texts/study guides
- ❏ Use supplementary materials
- ❏ Note-taking assistance
- ❏ Type teacher material
- ❏ Large print
- ❏ Special Equipment: ❏ electric typewriter ❏ computer
  - ❏ calculator ❏ phone adaptations ❏ video recorder
- ❏ Community Resources
- Other_____

Modifications for Planning A lesson planning pyramid focuses on identifying concepts to be taught by asking, "What do I want all, most, and some of the students to learn as a result of the lesson?" The form provides areas in which to record lesson format/teaching style, social/physical environment (conditions or lesson location), level of personal assistance, and in-class assignments/homework. In addition, there is an agenda, or instructional input, area to specify activities for the lesson. The lesson planning pyramid is designed to stand alone or complement your existing lesson plans.

To begin to plan effectively to incorporate curriculum and instructional modifications for students with exceptionalities into your classroom, it is helpful to compile an overview of the goals in the student's IEP "snapshot" in relationship to the breadth of your regular curriculum and general supports you have developed from the modification checklist. A daily scheduling matrix is a simple way to incorporate IEP goals from the IEP snapshot into the breadth of the regular curriculum covered in the activities of your class. The general supports and modifications needed by your student can be listed with check marks indicating when they are necessary during regular class activities.

Applied Case Study

A sample daily scheduling matrix was developed for Mark. Mark's specific IEP goals were listed and the daily class activities in which they will be addressed were indicated with check marks.

- The majority of Mark's IEP goals were met during the second-grade language arts class.

- The special educator co-taught and facilitated cooperative learning groups, peer tutoring, learning centers, and independent activities to assist Mark in achieving his specific goals and objectives.

- During other areas of the curriculum, Mark required both technical and physical supports to also ensure success. Technical supports included a tape recorder, an audio card reader and voice-activated computer programs.

DAILY SCHEDULING MATRIX

Student _____ Grade _____

Subject											
Time											

IEP Goals												
Breadth of Curriculum												
General Supports												

Form adapted from Giangreco, 1993

Sample Lesson Plan Pyramid

Date 11/5   Class Language Arts

Period 9-10:20   Unit/Topic Story Writing

Lesson Objective Given designated skill level, student will read, spell, and write words, sentences and stories emphasizing designated skill area. (Mark: short vowels)

Materials	Evaluation
Recipe to read charts, student journal, readers, tape recorder, computer learning centers' material.	Daily charts Teacher monitor of journal and reading
Delivery	**Level of Personal Assistance**
Teachers as facilitators, peer tutoring, cooperative learning groups, learning centers.	Teachers as facilitators, cooperative group interaction, peer tutors
Social/Physical Environment	**In Class/Homework**
Group tables Learning centers	Learning centers: skill practice Home: practice reading

	Pyramid	Agenda
What some students will learn	Read, write, spell individual letters and words at designed skill level.	10 min. Skill Builders Practice: Peer tutor listens to tutee read sounds or words. Chart. 15 min. Each group reviews designated new skills using visuals and music. 20 min. Groups write stories incorporating members' different skills. (Mark dictates and illustrates story.)
What most students will learn	Read, write, spell sentences at designed skill level.	2 min. Stretch 15 min. Learning centers (choice): Independently or cooperatively in small groups, students practice skills, e.g., audio card reader exercises, computer activities, etc.
What ALL students will learn	Read, write, spell stories at designed skill level. Write and read original stories; Minimum 5 sentences.	15 min. Students read stories. 2 min. Assign homework: Read word lists and stories.

Form adapted from Vaughn, Bos and Schumm, 1997

LESSON PLAN PYRAMID

Date _____ Class _____

Period _____ Unit/Topic _____

Lesson Objective _____

_____

_____

Materials	Evaluation
Delivery	**Level of Personal Assistance**
Social/Physical Environment	**In Class/Homework**

	Pyramid	Agenda
What some students will learn		
What most students will learn		
What ALL students will learn		

Form adapted from Vaughn, Bos and Schumm, 1997

Glossary of Terms As you are working with other professionals in the IEP meeting, there are many terms that may emerge. While most of these terms will be familiar to you, some may not. The following glossary may help you to more fully participate in these conversations or interpret them for parents.

Advocacy. One of the primary characteristics of the Individuals with Disabilities Education Act, which involves the assignment of representatives (advocates) for individuals with disabilities who lack parents or guardians.

Articulation disorders. Occur when students are unable to produce the sounds and sound combinations of language.

Attention Deficit Disorder (ADD). A disorder consisting of two subtypes of behavior; inattention and hyperactivity-impulsivity.

Audiogram. A visual representation of an individual's ability to hear sound.

Autism. A developmental disability characterized by extreme withdrawal and communication difficulties.

Blind. Describes an individual who is unable to see and, therefore, uses tactual (touch) and auditory (hearing) abilities to access the environment.

Cerebral palsy. Results from damage to the brain before or during birth; conditions are classified according to the areas affected and the types of symptoms.

Classwide Peer Tutoring. Students of different reading levels (one average or high, and one low) are paired and read materials that can be easily read by the least able reader in the pair.

Collaboration. A style for direct interaction between at least two co-equal parties voluntarily engaged in shared decision-making as they work toward a common goal.

Compensatory education. Instruction designed to compensate (make up) for prior lack of educational opportunities, and intervention or prevention programs.

Consultation model. An interactive process that enables people with diverse expertise to generate creative solutions to mutually defined problems.

Continuum of services. A full range of service options for students with disabilities, provided by the school system.

Cooperative learning groups. Groups of students work together toward a common goal, usually to help one another learn academic material.

Cooperative teaching. General and special education teachers work together to coordinate curriculum and instruction and teach heterogeneous groups of students in the general education classroom setting.

Co-planning. General and special education teachers work together to plan activities for students.

Creatively gifted or talented. Describes students who display their unique abilities within the framework of various forms of communication (drawing, music, singing, writing, and acting).

Cross-age pairing. A method of pairing older students with younger students for reading instruction.

Cross-categorical approach. Accommodations for exceptional learners are discussed in terms of students' shared needs rather than in terms of their identification as members of a disability category.

Deaf. Describes a person with a severe or profound loss of hearing.

Deafness-blindness. Also known as *dual sensory impairment;* involves impairments in the two main channels (auditory and visual) of receptive communication and learning.

Down Syndrome. One of the most common chromosomal disorders, usually associated with mental retardation.

Due process. Ensures that everyone with a stake in the student's educational success has a voice; also addresses written notification to parents for referral and testing for special education, parental consent, and guidelines for appeals and record keeping, education classrooms, resource rooms, special schools, and other types of settings.

Educational placement. The type of educational setting in which a particular student is instructed; examples include general education classrooms, resource rooms, special schools, and other types of settings.

Emotional or behavioral disorders. Behavior that falls considerably outside the norm.

Enrichment. Adding breadth and depth to the traditional curriculum.

Epilepsy. A condition characterized by the tendency to have recurrent seizures that are sudden, excessive, spontaneous, and abnormal discharges of neurons accompanied by alteration in motor function, and/or sensory function and/or consciousness.

Equity pedagogy. The teacher attends to different teaching and learning styles and modifies teaching to facilitate the academic achievement for students from diverse cultures.

Exceptionalities. Refers to students who represent a range of disability categories (e.g., students with emotional disorders, learning disabilities, physical impairments, and students who are gifted).

Fetal Alcohol Syndrome (FAS). Refers to a spectrum of birth defects caused by the mother's drinking during pregnancy.

Flexible grouping. The use of different student patterns that vary in composition, size, and frequency of meetings.

Free and Appropriate Public Education (FAPE). Mandatory legislation provides that all students with disabilities be given a free and appropriate public education.

Full inclusion. A movement that advocates educating all students with disabilities in the general education classroom full-time.

Giftedness. Evidence of high performance capability in areas such as intelligence, creativity, art, or leadership, or in specific academic fields, that requires services or activities not ordinarily provided by the school in order to more fully develop these capabilities.

Hard of hearing. Describes a person with a mild to moderate loss of hearing.

Hyperactivity. Refers to a group of behaviors associated with restlessness and excess motor activity.

Inclusion. The situation in which students with disabilities are educated with their non-disabled peers, with special education supports and services provided as needed.

Inclusion support teachers. A teacher whose responsibilities include supporting students with disabilities (e.g., mental retardation, severe disabilities, physical disabilities, visual impairments) in general education classrooms.

Individualized Education Program (IEP). A written plan, developed to meet the special learning needs of each student with disabilities.

Individuals with Disabilities Education Act (IDEA). Legislation designed to ensure that all students with disabilities receive an appropriate education through special education and related services.

Interactive planning. Involves monitoring students' learning and making adaptations in response to their needs.

Learning Disability. A condition present in students with average or above average potential intelligence who are experiencing a severe discrepancy between their ability and achievement in specific areas: reading, writing, spelling, language, or math.

Least Restrictive Environment (LRE). The instructional setting most like that of non-disabled peers that also meets the educational needs of each student with disabilities.

Legal blindness. Describes an individual who with the best possible correction in the better eye has a measured visual acuity of 20/200 or worse, or a visual field restricted to 20 degrees or less.

Lesson Planning Pyramid. A framework for lesson planning that helps teachers consider individual student needs within the context of planning for the class as a whole.

Mainstreaming. The participation of students with disabilities in general education classrooms to the extent appropriate for meeting their needs.

Mental retardation. Characterizes individuals who have limited intellectual functioning that affects their learning.

Multidisciplinary Team (MDT). This group of individuals usually includes a representative of the local education agency, the classroom teacher, the special education teacher, parents or guardians, and, when appropriate, the student, who together develop and implement the IEP.

Multiple disabilities. Describes individuals who have severe or profound mental retardation and one or more significant motor or sensory impairments and/or special health needs.

Multiple intelligences. Theory that human beings are capable of exhibiting intelligence in seven domains: linguistic, logical-mathematical, spatial, musical, bodily-kinesthetic, interpersonal (i.e., discerning and responding to the needs of others), and intrapersonal (i.e., having detailed and accurate self-knowledge).

Muscular Dystrophy (MD). A chronic disorder characterized by the weakening and wasting of the body's muscles.

Neurological impairment. A disability caused by a dysfunction of the brain, spinal cord, and nerves, thereby creating transmission of improper instruction, uncontrolled bursts of instructions from the brain, or incorrect interpretation of feedback to the brain.

Noncompliance. Failure to comply with the law; the Individuals with Disabilities Act requires that states mandate consequences for noncompliance.

Orthopedic impairment. Includes deficits caused by congenital anomaly (e.g., clubfoot, absence of some member), impairments caused by disease (e.g., poliomyelitis, bone tuberculosis) and impairments from other causes (e.g., cerebral palsy, amputation, and fractures or burns that cause contractures).

Other Health Impairments (OHI). Limited strength, vitality, or alertness (caused by chronic or acute health problems such as heart condition, tuberculosis, rheumatic fever, nephritis, asthma, sickle cell anemia, hemophilia, epilepsy, lead poisoning, leukemia, or diabetes) that adversely affects a student's educational performance.

Partial participation. A concept that assumes an individual has the right to participate, to the extent possible, in all activities.

Partially sighted. Describes an individual who with best possible correction in the better eye has a measured visual acuity between 20/70 and 20/200.

Peer Collaboration Model. Developed to help classroom teachers solve problems by providing time and structure to do so.

Peer tutoring. One student in a pair acts as a teacher for the other student.

Prereferral Assistance Team (PAT). A group of teachers from the same school who meet regularly to discuss the specific

progress of students brought to their attention by other teachers in the school.

Public Law 94-142. This legislation, designed to ensure that all students with disabilities receive an appropriate education through special education and related services, was originally referred to as the Education for All Handicapped Students Act, enacted in 1975, and later reauthorized and expanded as the Individuals with Disabilities Education Act (IDEA).

Pull-out Program. Programs in which students are literally pulled out of their general education classroom for supplemental instruction in basic skills.

Regular Education Initiative (REI). A concept that promotes coordination of services between regular and special education.

Related services. The types of services to which students with disabilities are entitled, including: speech therapy, ideology, psychological services, physical therapy, occupational therapy, recreation, early identification and assessment, counseling, medical services for diagnostic or evaluation purposes, school health services, transportation, and social work services.

Remediation. Additional instruction for students who do not demonstrate, at an expected rate, competency, in basic skills in reading, writing, and mathematics.

Special education resource room. A placement outside the general education classroom where students with disabilities receive specialized, individualized, and intensive instruction to meet their needs.

Specific learning disabilities. Represents a heterogeneous group of students who, despite adequate cognitive functioning and the ability to learn some skills and strategies quickly and easily, have great difficulty learning other skills and strategies.

Speech disorders. Disorders that involve unintelligible or unpleasant communication.

Spina bifida. A birth defect that occurs when the spinal cord fails to close properly.

Student Find. A requirement that each state identifies and tracks the number of students with disabilities and plan for their educational needs.

Students at risk. Students who fail to succeed academically and who require additional instruction.

Systems of support. Refers to the coordinated set of services and accommodations matched to the student's needs.

Teacher Assistance Team (TAT). A group of teachers who provide initial strategies and support for fellow classroom teachers prior to referring a student for assessment for special education services.

Transdisciplinary teaming. Refers to a group of experts working together and viewing the students as a whole instead of working independently in a single specialty area.

Traumatic brain injury. An injury to the brain, caused by an external physical force, that causes total or partial functional disability or psychosocial impairment, or both, which adversely affects a student's educational performance.

Tutoring. A systematic plan for supplementing the student's educational program.

Visual acuity. The clarity with which an individual can see an object from a distance of 20 feet.

Vocational Rehabilitation Act. This act (Public Law 93-112) prevents any private organization that uses federal funds, or any local or state from discriminating solely on the basis of those disabilities.

Zero reject. An element of IDEA that states no student with disabilities can be excluded from receiving a free and appropriate education.

Adapted from Vaughn, Bos and Schumn, 1997

DIFFERENTIATING FOR ENGLISH LANGUAGE LEARNERS

Diversity is an integral part of today's schools. According to the NCELA and NCTE, in 2003–2004 over five million English language learners were in schools within the United States. The number of students acquiring English as a second language as indicated by a survey in 2002, is estimated at 4,747,763. According to the 2000 U.S. Census, 47 million residents age five and older speak a language other than English in their homes.

Because of these statistics, it is very probable that you will teach in a classroom where at least some of the students are learning English as a second language. Research on second-language learning has shown that there are many misconceptions about how students learn languages. Teachers need to be aware of these research findings, and unlearn old ways of thinking. Language learning by school-aged students takes longer, is harder, and involves a great deal more struggle than most teachers have been led to believe. In order to successfully teach these students, it is important to first dispel some of the common myths regarding English language learning.

Myths About English Language Learning

Myth 1 When ELL students are able to converse comfortably in English, they have developed proficiency in the language.

Fact: Research has shown that it can take six to nine years for ELL students to achieve the same levels of proficiency in academic English as native speakers.

Myth 2 Any amount of native-language content instruction is detrimental for students who are non- or limited-English proficient (LEP).

Fact: LEP students who receive no instruction in their native language often develop a negative self-concept, and ultimately may drop out of school. There is a great deal of evidence that oral communication skills in a second language may be acquired within two or three years. But it may take up to four to six years to acquire the level of proficiency for understanding the language in its instructional uses.

Myth 3 In earlier times, immigrant students learned English rapidly and assimilated easily into American life.

Fact: Many immigrant students during the early part of this century did not learn English quickly or well. Many dropped out of school to work in jobs that did not require the kinds of academic achievement and communication skills that substantive employment opportunities require today.

Language Learning Programs There are many types of language programs that provide support for students. Many of these programs are driven by the politics of the state, rather than the needs of the students. Guest writer, Jeanne Fain, provides a brief overview of the current programs.

Grappling with Teaching Practice for Linguistically Diverse Learners
By Jeanne Fain, Ph.D.

There are several types of models that have been used historically and are currently being implemented, which include the following bilingual education programs and English language instructional programs (Peregoy & Boyle, 2005; Ovando & Collier, 1998).

Bilingual Education Programs

High quality bilingual programs purposely strive to honor and develop the student's first language and build upon the student's knowledge of his or her first language while introducing acquisition of English as a second language. Transitional bilingual programs traditionally serve English language learners for three years (Peregoy & Boyle, 2005). Typically these programs begin in kindergarten and students are exited into mainstream classrooms by third grade. The purpose of this program is to draw upon the student's first language as a bridge to learning literacy and academic content that moves learning along in English (Peregoy & Boyle, 2005). This model of bilingual education is often identified as subtractive bilingualism and the end result is for students to become monolinguals in English (Faltis, 2006). This type of program is utilized in schools that have large numbers of English language learners with the same home languages (Faltis & Hudelson, 1998).

Maintenance bilingual education is designed to serve English language learners by strengthening the development, acquisition and proficiency of their home language while simultaneously teaching a second language, which in most cases is oral and written English. Dual language programs or two-way immersion programs draw upon bilingual education and the Canadian immersion model. Many dual language programs explore the dimensions of society, culture and politics (Soltero, 2004). These programs focus on students becoming fully biliterate and bilingual in two languages. Usually classes consist of 50% of students fully proficient in a language other than English and the other 50% of the students are fully proficient in English. Instruction begins in the early grades with the language that is not English. English instruction is provided for students who are learning English as a second language.

English Language Instructional Programs

English language instructional programs include submersion, Pull-Out/Push-In, Sheltered English or Specially Designed Academic Instruction in English (SDAIE), and Structured English Immersion (Faltis, 2006). Submersion or commonly called sink or swim includes programs that focus on English language learners learning English quickly in a mainstream classroom and without support or changes in the curriculum. Pull-Out involves students learning outside of the classroom and students receive additional instructional assistance related to English language development regularly from an English Language Learner (ELL) teacher or assistant. Push-In is occurring more often in classrooms. The ELL teacher or assistant comes into the classroom and works on English language development within the classroom.

Sheltered English or Specially Designed Academic Instruction in English (SDAIE) is a program designed primarily to instruct students solely in English while simultaneously teaching content areas. This program works well for students who have intermediate English language proficiency and are secondary students (Faltis, 1993; Peregoy & Boyle, 2005). Sheltered instruction changes based upon linguistic needs made to instruction in terms of delivery, use of visuals, modified texts, and experiences (Echevarria & Graves, 2007).

Structured English Instruction (SEI) is legally mandated in states that have passed English Only laws such as California, Arizona, and Massachusetts. English language acquisition is where instruction is in English and there is minimal native language support. Students are expected learn English within a year. Classroom teachers have created and adopted various interpretations of SEI (Gandara, Maxwell-Jolly, Garcia, Asato, Gutierrez, Stritikus, Curry, 2000). Many teachers are in need of further clarification and research regarding the differences between SEI and mainstream sink or swim education (Wright & Choi, 2005).

Newcomer Programs have been created by some school districts for newly arriving immigrant students. These programs include beginning English language development along with content instruction and are geared for middle and secondary students. Some programs include support for families as they adapt to the United States (Ovando, Collier, & Combs, 2006).

Language Learning Principles The following section offers two major themes regarding English language learning. The first section deals with building positive attitudes toward the English language learner, and the second describes strategies that support English language learners.

Positive Attitudes Toward the English Language Learner

- **Have High Expectations**
  Students are natural acquirers of language. Expect them to become proficient in English. Most students have already acquired a first language successfully. All concepts and skills learned in their native language can easily be transferred to the second language.

- **Remember That Language Is a Process**
  English language learners start out in the silent stage, which may last from one day to a few months. They should not be forced to speak during this time but can follow comprehensible directions and listen to comprehensible stories, nursery rhymes, and songs. They will usually understand much more than they can express.

- **Take Time to Develop Good Rapport with Your Students**
  Students who have positive feelings about English and the people who speak English are more highly motivated to learn the language. Ask your students how to pronounce their names. Your ELL students will appreciate the respect and courtesy your efforts show. Try to learn something about the students' cultural backgrounds, which may make you more sensitive to unfamiliar behavior or responses.

- **Set a Cheerful Tone of Confidence in the Classroom**
  Students cannot learn effectively when they are anxious and upset. Acknowledge any evidence of learning. Take time to establish a supportive environment.

- **Find Ways That All Learners Can Experience Success with Language in Context**

  Students learn at different rates. Language aptitude, age, personality, and cultural and linguistic background all affect the rate and proficiency of language learning. Use gestures, facial expressions, demonstrations, and tone of voice to help students understand the message you are trying to convey. Bring in real objects and other visuals. Provide real-life, hands-on experiences for the students. English language learners take things very literally; so always check for understanding by asking specific questions.

Strategies That Support English Language Learners

- **Teach Language as It Is Really Used**

  Don't worry about such things as subjunctive or the difference between who and whom. Even native speakers misuse these, but are easily understood. You can help ELL students by using cognates whenever possible and basic words that have broad meanings.

  ### COGNATES

Spanish	English
honor	honor
tres	trio
pantalones	pants
rodeo	rodeo
jardin	garden
carro	car
color	color

- **Let Grammar Emerge from the Communication Goal**

  Teach grammar as it is needed for successful communication. Try not to teach it in isolation or for its own sake.

- **Don't Get Discouraged by Errors**

  An error does not necessarily mean that the student has not learned a particular language feature. There is usually a lag between understanding a particular language feature and the student's ability to use it.

- **Adapt Your Language to the Ability of Your Students**

  Although sentences should be grammatically correct, you can simplify structures, slow the pace, limit your vocabulary, speak clearly and control the use of obscure idioms. But keep the language natural. You may need to pause longer where you would normally pause in speaking or say important sentences in several different ways.

- **Accept Language Interference**

  Accented speech and some grammatical errors are inevitable for English language learners, and are acceptable as long as students can communicate effectively. The new language has been superimposed on an existing system; there is bound to be interference between the two.

- **Keep the Class Student-Centered**

  Develop opportunities for students to learn English by using it. Students should be talking while the teacher acts as a language guide.

- **Make Language Learning Incidental to Some Other Task**
  Do not spend an inordinate amount of time with drill and practice or learning vocabulary in isolation. Teach students important concepts and the vocabulary for those concepts the other students are learning.

- **Have Students Help Each Other Learn**
  Language is social. English language learners must have numerous opportunities for interacting with peers, especially proficient English speakers. Use cooperative learning, a buddy system, peer tutoring, or some other means to enable the more fluent students to help those who are non-native speakers of English. Use student pairs for team learning, especially for reports, experiments, and projects.

- **Vary Classroom Activities**
  Plan lessons in short segments and allow students to be actively engaged throughout the lesson. Develop thematic units to cover concepts and vocabulary in interesting, meaningful ways. Use students' literature, guests, and hands-on experiences to teach concepts and vocabulary. When having students practice, remember that massed practice promotes fast learning and distributed practice promotes lasting learning. If you want students to remember something for a long time, it must be practiced over and over again, gradually lengthening the amount of time between practice sessions.

- **Provide a Dramatic Play Center**
  A dramatic play center for primary students can mimic the home environment. Boxes of food, coupons, labels for utensils and dishes, pictures, and miniature appliances enable students to use their second language in a non-threatening situation. Teachers have found that students break their "silent period" more quickly during this type of pretend play.

- **Encourage Singing**
  Singing in the chorus gives the ELL student a chance to learn to pronounce strange new words in a risk-free activity. If the English songs are displayed on a chart and the teacher points to each word as it is sung, students receive an easy "reading" lesson.

Building Bridges with English Language Learners

Tips for Communicating with English Language Learners

1. Learn to pronounce the student's first and last name correctly.
2. Make your classroom a friendly place for parents of students from all cultures by including bulletin boards, class work, and information from around the world.
3. Have an English Language Learner resource teacher, bilingual teacher, or bilingual aide review the information you are sending to parents.
4. Learn a few words or phrases in the first language of your ELL students, for example: Bon Jour, Hola!, Guten Tag, or Bon Dia.
5. Allow your students to translate for their parents at conference and open houses. Tell the parents how much you enjoy teaching their son or daughter and encourage them to attend school functions and help in the classroom.
6. Use bilingual parents to translate for those parents who have not yet mastered English sufficiently to communicate with you.
7. Investigate the possibility of having an adult ELL class taught on your campus. This would help familiarize the parents with your campus and show them that we are all learning new skills.

Increasing Learning and Engagement There are several simple ways to support reading instruction for your ELL students. Since they probably are hearing and speaking the new language for the first time, they need additional practice listening to the second language. They will also need extra help with the books they are reading. Try these ideas:

- Support reading instruction by providing CD ROMs, videos, audiocassettes, and other materials that may be used independently or in small groups.
- Prepare difficult passages from textbooks on tape for listening.
- Maintain a library of supplementary books written in simple English that offer additional illustrations for problem areas.
- Highlight written materials for readability by enlarging the size of print, organizing chapters meaningfully, and highlighting the headings that show introductions for transition from one idea to another.

Other ways to increase motivation, aid in retention, and keep students on task are:

- Make material interesting and meaningful.
- Provide biographies of significant men and women from different cultures.
- Develop interest and arouse curiosity through hands-on experiences, the outdoors and simulations.
- Offer a variety of reference materials at the students' instructional level for independent use.
- Collect many of the comic books available that portray historic and cultural events in simplified language.

While students are learning a new language, they still need opportunities to be recognized and feel successful. Here are a few suggestions.

- Tape-record problems for independent listening assignments.
- Write instructions and problems that must be worked. If directions are written, ELL students can read the directions more than once, refer to them and show them to others who may be helping.
- Limit the number of problems that must be worked, the number of variables in lab experiments, or the number of questions to be answered. Consider allowing the students to give an oral report rather than a written one to demonstrate comprehension more accurately.
- De-emphasize speed and emphasize accuracy of work. English language learners need more time to process and produce their second language. They may need more time for a test, drawings, charts, and gestures until they have adequate second language acquisition.
- Teach selectively. Be clear about what is important; teach to the objective. Separate important points from periphery information.
- Include frequent checks for comprehension. Dialogue between you and your students can alert you to avoid confusion and misunderstanding. Ask a question that requires all students to demonstrate their understanding of a concept. This practice will also force students to stay on task and be involved in their learning.
- Allow for multiple ways to demonstrate their comprehension. Oral language is just one form of expression. ELL students can also demonstrate their understanding of concepts through artistic expression.

Instructional Resources and Technology

Effective teachers use a wide variety of materials to teach their students the content to be learned. They know that nearly all students do better if they can be exposed to content in a variety of ways. For example: you will want to use technology, software, audio-visual materials, community resources, equipment, manipulatives, library resources, local guest speakers, and volunteers.

In addition to basic classroom supplies, you need to know how to locate specific instructional resources that are available through the district. Most districts have a media or curriculum center that is a repository for materials that are shared across schools. The district media/curriculum center usually offers a range of instructional videotapes, DVD's, computer software, CD-ROM discs and audiocassettes for every subject that is taught. Ask district staff development personnel for a brief tour of this facility. You will also want to learn how to check out instructional materials and equipment, and inquire about the length of time materials can be loaned.

After you have reviewed the district's resources, consider other sources of material, such as discount teacher supply companies that will send catalogs of their merchandise. In addition to buying materials, you will soon discover that many of your colleagues frequent garage sales, thrift stores, and even junkyards in their quest for teaching resources! Experienced teachers regularly find wonderful, interesting, and inexpensive supplies, resources, and classroom furniture and equipment at these places.

Another fabulous resource for teachers is the Internet. Following is a list of websites that offer a wide range of instructional materials that you may browse through from the comfort of a home computer. There are thousands of websites for teachers but here are a few favorites.

WEBSITES

http://www.yahoo.com/Education/K_12/
Yahoo site for Pre-K-12 education resources. Yahoo is one of the major search engines on the Internet that will take searchers to a wealth of educational materials and resources.

http://www.yahoo.com/Recreation/Travel/Virtual_Field_Trips/
Links to virtual field trips of Pre-K-12 interest. Many are interactive and include lesson plans.

http://www.ed.gov
For access to the U.S. Department of Education homepage to access current information in education and to access ED-funded Internet resources.

http://www.kdp.org
Offers a wealth of insights on topics of interest for teachers. Offers publications viewable online, and teacher resources by topic.

http://www.education.usatoday.com
Offers interactive projects and global education resources for educators, students, and parents.

http://www.whitehouse.gov/sh/welcome.htm
Posts the newsletter, *The Whitehouse for Kids*, which includes current information about government and the happenings of the White House.

best PRACTICES

This study asked students to state their preference for an objectivist or a constructivist learning environment and consider the consequent implications for their role as a learner. They did this by identifying with the dialogue depicted in two concept cartoons. Results indicate an overwhelming preference among students for a constructivist learning environment. This suggests not only that students would be receptive to moves by teachers towards more constructivist principles in the classroom, but also that a failure to promote such a transition may contribute to an epistemological gap between teaching and learning styles that will be an impediment to meaningful learning. Students anticipated constructivist learning environments would be more interesting, more effective at developing students' understanding and would permit them to take greater ownership of their learning.

Kinchin, I.M. (2004, Winter). Investigating students' beliefs about their preferred role as learners. *Educational Research, 46*(3), 301–312.

Questions for Reflection

Student Engagement

- How will you keep students engaged?
- How will you systematically group students?
- How will you use peer-tutoring?

Differentiated Instruction

- How will you refer a student for additional support?
- How will you use an Individualized Education Plan (IEP) to meet student needs?
- How will you manage student modifications?
- How will you meet the needs of English language learners?

evaluation QUESTIONS

- How will you engage students in the learning process?
- How will you differentiate instruction to support student needs?

Self-Assessment of Professional Growth

Name				Date	
Grade Level/Content Area					

Instructional Planning	Low				High
To what degree do I have the knowledge needed for organizing lesson planning for effective instruction?	1 ☐	2 ☐	3 ☐	4 ☐	5 ☐
To what degree do I have the teaching skills needed for organizing lesson planning for effective instruction?	1 ☐	2 ☐	3 ☐	4 ☐	5 ☐
Curriculum Integration	Low				High
To what degree do I have the knowledge needed for effectively incorporating curriculum integration?	1 ☐	2 ☐	3 ☐	4 ☐	5 ☐
To what degree do I have the teaching skills needed for effectively incorporating curriculum integration?	1 ☐	2 ☐	3 ☐	4 ☐	5 ☐
Student Engagement	Low				High
To what degree do I have the knowledge needed for engaging students in the learning process?	1 ☐	2 ☐	3 ☐	4 ☐	5 ☐
To what degree do I have the teaching skills needed for engaging students in the learning process?	1 ☐	2 ☐	3 ☐	4 ☐	5 ☐
Differentiated Instruction	Low				High
To what degree do I have the knowledge needed to effectively differentiate instruction to support needs?	1 ☐	2 ☐	3 ☐	4 ☐	5 ☐
To what degree do I have the teaching skills needed to effectively differentiate instruction to support needs?	1 ☐	2 ☐	3 ☐	4 ☐	5 ☐

Next Steps

Set goals for next steps to implement best practices in the teaching standards of instructional design and instruction.

_____

_____

_____

_____

_____

_____

_____

_____

_____

_____

_____

_____

_____

_____

_____

_____

_____

_____

_____

_____

_____

Assessment: Managing Student Progress

4

> **"** Assessment is the process of observing, recording, and documenting the work students do and how they do it, for the purpose of making sound educational decisions for each individual student. **"**
>
> —JARDINE

Today the demands of accountability for national and state standards, district goals and grade level objectives are uppermost in mind for administrators and teachers. No Child Left Behind Act (NCLB) has defined what students at each grade level should know and do.

Today states ensure that these standards impact teachers' instruction and curriculum decisions by administering annual standardized achievement tests, as mandated by NCLB. Each school must meet annual yearly progress goals, with 100 percent of the school's students "meeting the standards" in reading and mathematics by the 2013–2014 school year.

While student progress is measured on standardized tests that occur annually, effective teachers assess student progress continually. This chapter offers practical ways to collect data and measure student progress. As the students interpret and apply new information, teachers can determine what was clear to students and what needs to be re-taught or refined. Teacher instruction, student learning, and assessment are continuously intertwined activities.

POINTS OF INQUIRY

- How will you use varying measures to assess student learning?
- How will you use assessment to guide ongoing instruction?
- How will you document student growth and development?
- How will you report student learning?

Establishing a Comprehensive Assessment System

❝ Maybe the most any of us can expect of ourselves isn't perfection but progress. **❞**

—MICHELLE BURFORD

Evaluating Student Learning

What is good work? As a teacher you may find evaluating student accomplishments among the most thought-provoking decisions you make. Your greatest challenge will be to create a comprehensive assessment system that:

- allows students multiple ways to reveal their unique abilities and talents;
- involves students in assessing their progress and establishing learning goals;
- presents a total picture of the student's social and intellectual growth;
- is fair and reflective of the local and national norms of student achievement;
- parents and administrators understand and respect.

The purpose of this section is to offer a number of suggestions about how to establish a comprehensive assessment system and begin the process of documenting student achievement. A comprehensive assessment system:

- Provides teachers with opportunities to determine the effectiveness of their instruction by observing how students interpret and apply new information.
- Considers multiple sources of information and a variety of assessment measures when determining a student's abilities in different content areas.
- Teaches students how to assess and become involved in their own learning.
- Uses both on-demand (formal) and ongoing (informal) assessment measures to evaluate student progress.
- Allows teachers to modify their instruction based on student performance.

■■■ © 2008 Jupiter Images Corporation.

Types of Measures and Assessments

FORMATIVE AND SUMMATIVE ASSESSMENTS

Assessments, either professional or teacher-made, can be categorized into two broad types: **formative** and **summative**. Although these assessments may look identical, they serve different purposes.

- *Formative*—an assessment which measures the student's progress during a set of lessons or learning experiences. The teacher can provide appropriate feedback and help the student correct errors or misunderstanding and continue to meet learning objectives.
- *Summative*—an assessment used at the end of a learning unit to measure the progress the student has made over time. These assessments measure what the student was expected to know or do at the culmination of a unit of study.

For example, the weekly spelling list may be given to the class to study on Monday. They take a formative test on Wednesday, which informs the teacher and the students what they are to study. On Friday, the class takes the summative spelling test. The results of the Friday spelling test are recorded in the grade book and become a part of the spelling grade.

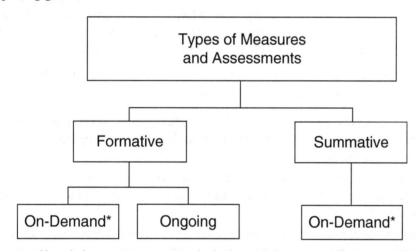

* Although these assessments may look identical, they serve different purposes.

ON-DEMAND ASSESSMENT

On-demand assessment includes norm-referenced, standardized, or criterion-referenced tests. Created by professionals, these types of tests, usually administered once or twice a year, are designed to indicate to teachers, parents, and administrators how much a student achieved compared to other students of the same age or grade level. These tests focus on group performance rather than on the achievement of an individual student. However, most parents believe this information is critical. Teachers need to be able to explain to parents how these tests are used and how to interpret the scores.

- *Norm-referenced test*—a test designed to compare one group of students with another group.
- *Standardized test*—a test in which the teacher reads a verbatim script of procedures to the students. The conditions and directions are the same whenever the test is administered.

- *Criterion-referenced test*—a test used to compare a student's progress toward mastery of specified content. The performance criterion is referenced to some criterion such as a cut-off score of mastery.

ONGOING ASSESSMENT

Ongoing assessment relies on the regular collection of products that demonstrate each student's knowledge and learning. This information immediately informs the teacher about how well students learned from the day's instruction. In addition, these assessments inform and guide the teacher's day-to-day instructional decisions. This category of assessment includes:

- student products, such as written stories, spelling tests
- observations, anecdotal notes and vignettes
- checklists of target skills
- video and audio tapes
- diagnostic or placement tests, such as a running record
- on-demand tests.

While teachers do not use all of these information-gathering tools in every lesson, each tool does provide unique and important information about what the students are learning and how effective the instruction has been. Therefore, it is important to incorporate each of these tools systematically as a lesson unit is planned.

Teacher Observations Teacher observation records include labeling, dating, and organizing documented student development over time.

- Anecdotal records—sometimes called unstructured observation. The teacher records student interactions with peers, print, literature, writing process, in-class discussion, center activities, etc.
- Checklists—sometimes called structured observation. The teacher uses predetermined observation guides to document student development and progress on specific skills or concepts.
- Vignettes—sometimes called teacher reflections. The teacher recalls student interactions and records them after the event has occurred.

Anecdotal Records These are a teacher's notes describing a student's behavior. Teachers often find it helpful to focus on a series of questions like the following:

- What can this student do?
- What does this student know?
- What does the student's attitude reveal about his/her growth and progress?

It is helpful for a teacher to select a focus and then make notes based on this focus for the course of a week. For example, in reading, teachers might focus on how fluently the students are reading, how well the students are comprehending the text, or student interest in reading as reflected in their free-choice book selections. Many teachers begin note-taking by focusing on those students whose progress is most concerning.

Some teachers use 2"×4" mailing labels and print out student names and week on the labels each week. Some teachers even type in the prompt or weekly focus on the labels. During the week, it is easy then for a teacher to see who he or she has observed and what students still need to be documented. At the end of the week the teacher transfers the label to each student's portfolio. Taken regularly, anecdotal notes become not only a vehicle for planning instruction and documenting progress, but also a story about each student's growth and development over time.

Checklists These are observational aids that specify which behaviors to look for and provide a convenient system for keeping records. They can make observations more systematic and easier to conduct, and can be used in a variety of instructional contexts. Checklists are useful because they provide lists of items that teachers can see at a glance, showing what students can do. Hence, teachers are careful to record the date of each observation and to use the checklists many times over the year in an attempt to create an accurate picture of student progress.

Sample Weekly Labels

Ariel Nov 12–16 Book Selection Expository text on Chicks—from Egg to Chick	Bonita Nov 12–16 Book Selection
Carrie Nov 12–16 Book Selection	Daren Nov 12–16 Book Selection Book—If You Give a Moose a Muffin Reading text easily

Vignettes or Teacher Reflections These are recordings or recollections of significant events made after the fact, when the teacher is free of distractions. Because vignettes are like anecdotal notes except that they are prepared some time after a behavior has occurred and are based on a teacher's memory of the event, vignettes are used for purposes such as those identified for anecdotal notes. These after-the-fact descriptions or vignettes can be more detailed than anecdotal notes and are particularly useful when recording behavior that is significant or unique for a specific student. For example, Ms. Jones observed one of her students attempting to control his peers' behavior by writing a sign and posting it in an appropriate place. Because she was involved with a small group of students, she did not have time to record a description of the student's behavior immediately. However, as soon as the students left for the day, she recorded her recollection of the event.

Sample Vignette

Manuel 3/7

For days, Manuel had been complaining about sharing his birthday gift (a soccer ball) with his friends during recess. Today, he wrote a note that said, "Pla bll wf Manuel, sin up." (Play ball with Manuel. Sign up.)

   He posted his sign on the door. This was the first time I had observed him using writing in an attempt to communicate.

In Practice: Video and Audio Recording Teachers often use audiotaping to document students' progress. To assess student reading ability, for example, teachers record their students' reading orally. Teachers use videotaping to capture student behaviors in a variety of contexts. Some teachers focus the camera lens on an area of the classroom, such as the dramatic-play area or on cooperative work groups, to gather information about the students' literacy-related and/or social interactions during their play and work. Viewing of the tapes provides valuable information, not only about the students' academic ability but also their ability to engage in social and functional conversations with others.

Interviews/Questions Techniques Interviews may be conducted with the student, parents, and special area teachers. Interviews may occur informally during the school day or may be formalized when the teacher needs to narrow the focus of the questions to reflect a previously identified concern. Teachers may consider four types of interview questions:

- Descriptive—What did you do during . . . ?
- Structured—Can you tell me when . . . ?
- Contrast—How are these stories alike/different?
- Process—How did you decide to . . . ?

Student Self-Assessment Techniques Students should be actively involved in assessing their own work, reflecting upon their progress, and establishing new learning goals. The following tools can be used to engage students in self-assessment.

- Teacher-made Questionnaires/Surveys
- Teacher-Student Conferences
- Rubrics
- Student Self-Assessments

■ © Terrie L. Zeller 2008. Used under license from Shutterstock, Inc.

STUDENT SELF-ASSESSMENT

Name _____ Teacher _____

Subject _____ Period _____ Date _____

The student completes the evaluation. Afterward, student and teacher discuss the accomplishments made by the student, decide on areas that need to be improved, and plan goals for future learning experiences.

O = Outstanding   S = Satisfactory   N = Needs Improvement

Student Self-Evaluation

_____ I completed all readings and assignments on time.
_____ I showed responsibility by bringing all appropriate materials to class.
_____ I showed growth in my planning and organizational skills.
_____ I have gained skills in doing research.
_____ I have gained skills in taking notes to gather information.
_____ I used a variety of relevant resources to learn about my subject.
_____ I improved my ability to analyze data.
_____ I gained confidence in my ability to synthesize information.
_____ I gained independence in working on my own to achieve a goal.
_____ I am able to evaluate my own accomplishments fairly.
_____ I identified what I need to improve, with accuracy and honesty.

The most important thing I learned was:

Regarding my work, I am most proud of:

Teacher/Student Conference

Accomplishments:

Area(s) for Improvement:

Goal(s):

Products, Work Samples, and Artifacts Teacher collects multiple examples of student-created products to assess each student's development. Some products, such as samples of student writing, can be gathered together in a folder. If the students' original works cannot be saved (e.g., an art project), a photograph can be made of the product. Because memories are short, the teacher or the student should record a brief description of the product or the activity that resulted in the product. For example:

- Journal Entries
- Learning Logs
- Formal Written Assignments
- Portfolios
- Student Presentations

In Practice: Portfolio Management System A portfolio allows the teacher to document a student's progress over time, and share that information with the student, the student's parents, and other teachers and administrators. The teacher devises a management system to collect and analyze samples of student work, teacher's anecdotal notes, and formal and informal assessment measures.

Many teachers find that folders with pockets and center clasps for three-hole-punched paper serve as better storage containers than file folders. Interview forms, running-record sheets, and other assessments can be three-hole-punched, thus permitting their easy insertion into each student's folder. When anecdotal notes and vignettes are written on computer mailing labels, the labels can be attached to the inside covers of each student's folder. When these notes are written on index cards, the cards can be stored in one of the folder's pockets. Also, a sealed sandwich bag could be stapled inside each student's folder to securely hold an audiotape. The class folders might be housed in a plastic container or in hanging files in a file cabinet.

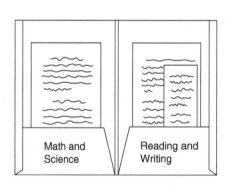

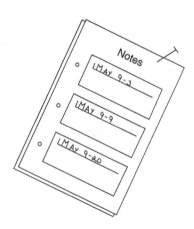

Determining What to Assess

An effective teacher must first determine the learner outcomes (sometimes called lesson objectives). This is the term educators use to describe what the students need to know and do by the end of the lesson.

Learner outcomes usually contain an observable verb such as recall, solve, measure, or construct, which allows the teacher to be able to determine the student comprehension and level of involvement at given points in the lesson. For example:

The student will be able to:

- define the term "photosynthesis";
- label the parts of an insect;
- calculate the diameter of a circle.

Learner outcomes that are clearly stated help make student progress easier to determine. In addition, clear learner outcomes allow measurement of student knowledge of a topic or subject at different levels. This comes from the major idea of the taxonomy, which is that educational objectives can be arranged in a hierarchy from less to more complex. Bloom's Taxonomy provides a range of educational objectives, verbs that reflect student knowledge level, questions that would typically elicit the level of response, and possible outcomes that would reflect that particular level of learning.

Dr. Bloom and his colleagues identified three broad categories of performance: affective, psychomotor, and cognitive learning.

- Affective learning is demonstrated by behaviors indicating attitudes of awareness, interest, attention, concern and responsibility; ability to listen and respond in interactions with others; and the ability to demonstrate those attitudinal characteristics or values that are appropriate to the test situation and the field of study.

- Psychomotor learning is demonstrated by physical skills such as coordination, dexterity, manipulation, grace, strength, and speed—actions that demonstrate the fine motor skills (such as use of precision instruments or tools) or actions which evidence gross motor skills (such as the use of the body in dance or athletic performance).

- Cognitive learning is the ability "to think things through." Cognitive objectives revolve around knowledge, comprehension, and application of any given topic.

There are multiple types of measurements that assess student understanding. The following presents Bloom's Taxonomy, with a list of observable outcomes that a teacher might choose as assessment measures.

Mentor Voices

➤ "Managing the data you collect is not difficult if you use student helpers and a user-friendly filing system. Student code numbers are extremely helpful, and save hours of time."

Characteristics and Outcomes of Bloom's Taxonomy

Level with Characteristics	Examples of Measurable Verbs	Outcomes
Knowledge: Can recognize and recall specific terms, facts, and symbols.	■ Count, Define, Draw, Identify, Indicate, List, Name, Point, Quote, Recall, Recite, Recognize, Record, Repeat, State, Tabulate, Trace, Write	■ Label a given diagram ■ Generate a list ■ Complete a quiz
Comprehension: Can understand the main idea of material heard, viewed, or read.	■ Associate, Compare, Compute, Contrast, Describe, Differentiate, Discuss, Distinguish, Estimate, Interpret, Predict, Translate	■ Write summary report ■ Oral retelling
Application: Applies an abstract idea in a concrete situation, or solves a problem or relates it to prior experiences.	■ Apply, Calculate, Classify, Compete, Demonstrate, Employ, Examine, Illustrate, Practice, Relate, Solve, Use	■ Produce illustration or diagram/map/model ■ Describe analogy or solve problems ■ Teach others
Analysis: Examines a concept and determines its major components, sees the connections—cause-effects, similarities-differences.	■ Analyze, Construct, Detect, Explain, Group, Infer, Order, Separate, Summarize, Utilize, Transform	■ Graph, survey, chart, diagram ■ Report showing cause-effect
Synthesis: Combines elements in new and original ways.	■ Arrange, Combine, Construct, Create, Design, Develop, Formulate, Generalize, Integrate, Organize, Plan, Prepare, Prescribe, Produce, Propose, Specify	■ Artwork—song, poem, dance, music, play, speech, video, film ■ Inventions—computer programs
Evaluation: Makes informed judgments about the value of ideas or materials.	■ Appraise, Assess, Critique, Determine, Evaluate, Grade, Judge, Measure	■ Debate/discussion ■ Letter to editor ■ Ranking

Adapted from Bloom, 1984

Assessing What Students Have Learned

When students are assessed as part of the teaching-learning process, the assessment information tells teachers what each student knows and can do, and what he or she is ready to learn next. Teachers also use their assessment of student learning to reflect on their own teaching practices so they can adjust and modify curricula, instructional activities, and classroom routines that are ineffective. The following are questions teachers need to consider when determining how and when they will assess student progress.

■ When should the teacher assess student progress?

Student understanding should be assessed at significant points throughout the entire lesson. This includes constant monitoring of student performance or occasionally pausing the lesson to ask all students to demonstrate their understanding of the information being taught.

- How can the teacher determine if all students can perform correctly?

  Beyond observation, the teacher may ask students to write the answer, tell a neighbor, respond in unison, indicate the answer individually, signal the answer or demonstrate the skill.

- Why should teachers assess students frequently?

  Before the teacher proceeds from one goal to the next, all students need to demonstrate an understanding of the content presented. If all students do not understand the lesson, the teacher will need to adjust teaching strategies, reteach, and then re-assess student progress to determine understanding before moving on to the next objective.

- How do teachers collect information about student progress?

  In addition to instructional strategies, effective teachers use a variety of tools to gather information about their students. Teachers then use the information when planning future lessons, and/or for making accommodations for students who are struggling. These tools can include: observations, interviews, student self-assessment, student artifacts, portfolios, quizzes, and tests.

Assessment in Action

Let's take a look at how some of these processes might look in a classroom.

Ms. Hope's first grade class just started a unit on life cycles. The lesson will cover a three-month time span in which the students will actually observe frog eggs as they develop into tadpoles that then evolve into frogs. Today she is beginning the overview of the unit and the lesson objective is: Students will be able to sequence the five stages of a frog's life cycle. To begin the lesson Ms. Hope asks the students to look at the cover of the book, The *Life Cycle of a Frog* by Ruth Thomson. She asks the students to begin to think about what they know about frogs. As the students respond she writes down their answers.

Sample KWL

What We <u>K</u>now	What We <u>W</u>ant to Learn	What We <u>L</u>earned
■ Frogs live in the water ■ Frogs hatch from eggs ■ Frogs are usually green ■ Frogs eat insects	■ What do baby frogs look like? ■ How long does it take for frog to grow up? ■ How long does it take for the eggs to hatch?	

Adapted from Bloom, 1984

Ms. Hope congratulates the students on their good questions. She begins reading the book. Most of the students do not realize that the eggs did not hatch into tiny frogs! The students are surprised to see that the eggs hatched into tadpoles. As student questions are answered, Ms. Hope says, "Let's remember that fact!" She also asks questions and draws their attention to the different stages of frog development.

After the story, Ms. Hope asks the students to retell the story sequence. She has created several magnet board pieces that illustrate the five stages of the frog's life cycle. The students work with her to organize the pieces in order. As they place them in order, the students also respond to Ms. Hope's question, "How long did it take for the eggs to hatch?" When they respond, she writes the information the students share on the magnetized whiteboard.

After the students have completed the retelling, Ms. Hope returns to the KWL chart and the students begin to raise their hands eagerly to add to the Learned column.

Sample Completed KWL

What We Know	What We Want to Learn	What We Learned
■ Frogs live in the water ■ Frogs hatch from eggs ■ Frogs are usually green ■ Frogs eat insects	■ What do baby frogs look like? ■ How long does it take for frog to grow up? ■ How long does it take for the eggs to hatch?	■ Baby frogs are first tadpoles! ■ It takes about 3 weeks for the eggs to hatch into a tadpole. ■ The tadpole takes about 12 to 16 weeks to grow into a frog. ■ Tadpoles have gills. ■ Tadpoles grow legs. ■ Tadpoles lose their tails.

Finally, Ms. Hope gives them a worksheet. The students write and label the steps. This product is individual confirmation of what the students have learned.

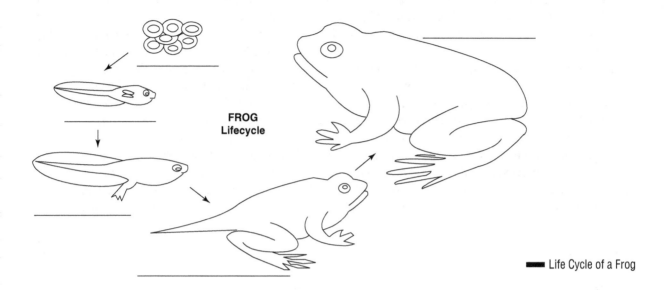

FROG Lifecycle

Life Cycle of a Frog

As we review Ms. Hope's lesson let's look at it in terms of assessment. She began her lesson with a clearly stated lesson objective: Students will be able to sequence the five stages of a frog's life cycle. To begin the lesson she activated student prior knowledge by introducing the book and asking the students to think about what they already knew about frogs.

Next, she asked the students to think about what they wanted to know about a frog's life cycle. This action increases student interest and focuses their attention on the objective. As she read the text, she kept asking questions and also connected student questions to the answers being discussed in the text. The questions she asked were also focused on the lesson objective.

At the end of the text, she asked the students to participate in the sequencing, labeling and discussion of the frog's life stages. This large group activity was both a review and practice for the individual assessment the students were being asked to complete. To reinforce their new knowledge they completed the What We Learned column of the KWL chart.

Finally, the students completed the worksheet, which provided an observable way for Ms. Hope to assess each student's knowledge of the different life stages of a frog. Tomorrow Ms. Hope will bring in the fresh-water aquarium to begin to hatch the frog eggs. Then, the students can begin the process of observing and documenting the developmental life cycle of the frogs. She can begin this activity knowing she has established a strong vocabulary and foundation for further learning.

PLANNING INSTRUCTION BASED ON ONGOING STUDENT ASSESSMENT

The following scenario demonstrates how one preschool teacher, Mr. Gleason, determines instructional activities based on the literacy standards, designs an authentic assessment as part of the instructional activity, then how he uses this information in a classroom performance matrix to help him determine further instruction for individuals and for the class as a whole. Finally, we can see how he develops a student portfolio to document individual student growth.

As Mr. Gleason plans his lessons, he also considers how his 18 young pre-kindergarten students will be able to demonstrate their new knowledge. For the past month, he has introduced six alphabet letters and sounds, using many exciting activities to help the students become alphabet detectives and sound sleuths. During this week, he has organized a letter center activity that not only reinforces these new skills, but also serves as an authentic assessment of student knowledge. To accomplish this goal, he plans to have the students do a letter hunt using environmental print coupons and labels that the students (and their parents) have collected. He has created a worksheet to help document student effort. The students are to sort through the pile of coupons until they find the target letters and then they will glue them in the appropriate row. Mr. Gleason or his aide are a part of this center and also make notes on student actions as they complete this assignment. The notes are collected over the course of the week as the students rotate through the centers during class, and then are transferred onto the Alphabet Matrix. The information from the matrix allows Mr. Gleason to see at a glance which student knows what letters, and then determine what and who needs further instruction.

Notice that Mr. Gleason is accomplishing several language and literacy standards, including:

- Listening Comprehension
    - Listens with increased attention.
    - Understands simple oral directions.

- Letter Knowledge and Early Word Recognition
    - Begins to associate letter names with their shapes.
    - Identifies ten or more printed letters.
    - Begins to notice beginning letters in familiar words.
    - Begins to make some letter sound matches.

- Written Expression
    - Attempts to connect the sounds in a words with its letter forms.

Likewise, since this is a social activity, Mr. Gleason will be able to relay how well each student is working with their peers.

■ © PhotoCreate 2008. Used under license from Shutterstock, Inc.

ALPHABET ACTIVITY-ASSESSMENT

Name _____ Date _____

Please write the letter name in the box. Find pictures and words that start with this letter. Glue the pictures and words in the row neatly.

B	
F	
P	

Sample Alphabet Activity-Assessment

Name __Annie__   Date _____

Please write the letter name in the box. Find pictures and words that start with this letter. Glue the pictures and words in the row neatly.

B		
F		
P		

Applied Case Study

Annie's activity-assessment page will be placed in her progress portfolio to document her progress over time. For example, an earlier version of this assessment only had three letters, but the next version of this assessment will have 9, then 12. Mr. Gleason selects the letters to be included on the assessment based on new letters he has presented and specific target letters that provided a challenge for the students initially. His assessment of the students provides immediate feedback about the effectiveness of past lessons and helps him to design new lessons for tomorrow.

ALPHABET MATRIX

Student	#	B	F	P	T	M	R	Comments
Annie	1	+	+	+	+	+	+	Great improvement on printing letters.
	2	+	+	+	+	+	+	Recognizes letters in words—even some lower case.
	3	+	+	+		+	+	Knows most of the letter sounds.
								Followed directions well.
								Shared materials easily with peers.
Briar	1	+	+	+	+	+	+	Prints letters extremely well, rapidly.
	2	+	+	+	+	+	+	Recognizes all letters.
	3	+	+	+			+	Letter sounds are improving.
								Followed directions.
								Shared materials.
Callie	1	+	+	+	+	+	+	Enjoys printing letters; form is improving.
	2		+	+	+	+	+	Knows most of the letter names.
	3		+	+				Still needs additional work time with letter sounds.
								Had difficulty following directions.
								Shared materials.

Key:

1. Student wrote the letter correctly.
2. Student recognizes letter immediately.
3. Student knows the letter sound.

Applied Case Study

Currently Mr. Gleason uses a simple worksheet to compile this information, but he is learning how to collect this same information on his laptop using an Excel spread sheet. This approach allows him to manipulate the data easily and produce immediate class reports and individual progress reports.

New Instructional Goals: What this simple assessment/learning activity demonstrated to Mr. Gleason was that although most of his students knew the letters and their names, they were still learning the letter sounds. This caused him to add an additional letter-sound game to his lesson plans and to ask his aide to work more closely at the writing center to demonstrate and reinforce letter-writing and letter sounds. Likewise, during shared writing time, he decided to take a few moments to highlight the features of target letters.

RUBRIC ASSESSMENT

Rubrics help guide students to perform based on specific expectations and provide a clear tool for teachers to assess based on those expectations. Following are samples of rubrics that can be used for a literature review and research summary, 3-D model/ diagram assessment, and student presentation for any content area.

Clearly, authentic assessment of young students is the best indication of what they actually know and can do, but it is important for the teacher to be able to document this information to share with directors, colleagues, and parents.

LITERATURE REVIEW AND RESEARCH SUMMARY RUBRIC

Name _____ Teacher_____

Subject _____ Period _____ Date _____

This is a record of research skills demonstrated by the student. The student initials, verifying completion, and the teacher's score indicates the degree to which the skill was successfully demonstrated. It is the student's task to bring this form and the documentation to the teacher for review.

Student Initial	Teacher Score	Research Skill
	/5	Located a book on the research topic. Cite book.
	/5	Used Internet to find three research articles on the research topic.
	/5	Summarized (1 page) each research article. Citations are included.
	/5	Wrote summary (2 paragraphs) interpreting graph, chart, or diagram relevant to the research topic. Graph, chart, or diagram is attached.
Total	**/20**	Comments:

3-D MODEL/DIAGRAM SCORING RUBRIC

Name _____ Teacher_____

Subject _____ Period _____ Date _____

The student and teacher will evaluate the diagram or model. The student assigns an:

O = Outstanding   S = Satisfactory   N = Needs Improvement.

The teacher will assign a score of 0–4 for a total possible score of 20.

Student Self-Assessment	Focus of Assessment	Teacher Assessment
	Elements of the model or diagram are accurate in shape.	/4
	Elements of the model or diagram are accurate in scale.	/4
	Labeling is accurate and legible.	/4
	Legend is accurate and legible.	/4
	Model or diagram is visually interesting and pleasing.	/4
Comments:		**/20 Total**

PRESENTATION RUBRIC

Name _____   Teacher_____

Subject _____   Period _____   Date _____

Presentation Requirements	Criteria	Points
Introduction	Provided an engaging introduction with accurate information about the topic. Comments:	/5
Content	Adequately covered the presentation topic in an organized manner with accurate information, referencing specific areas of information. Comments:	/5
Summary	Summarized findings and provided a meaningful closure. Comments:	/5
Presentation Skills	Consistently engaged audience, spoke with a loud and clear voice, completed presentation in allotted time. Comments:	/5
Total		**/20**

Black and Williams (1998) meta-analysis reviewed 20 quantitative studies (ranging in classroom ages from Kindergarten to university undergraduate) over several countries. The meta-analysis found that improved formative assessment (frequent assessment feedback to students from teachers) helps low achievers and students with special needs, more than other students and so reduces the range of achievement while raising achievement overall. A conclusion from this study suggested teachers should use frequent assessments to guide their instruction and ultimately improve student learning.

Black, P., & William, D. (1998). Inside the black box: Raising standards through classroom assessment. *Phi Delta Kappan, 80*(2), 139–148.

evaluation QUESTIONS

- How will you use varying measures to assess student learning?
- How will you use assessment to guide ongoing instruction?

Questions for Reflection

MEASURES FOR ASSESSMENT

- How will you use formative assessments to measure student progress?
- How will you use summative assessments to summarize student achievement?

ON-DEMAND AND ONGOING ASSESSMENTS

- How will you use on-demand assessments in your teaching practice?
- How will you explain to parents the difference between a norm-referenced, standardized and criterion-referenced test?
- How will you embed ongoing assessments within your lessons?

Record Keeping

“Never discourage anyone who continually makes progress no matter how slow.”

—PLATO

Report Cards

In your years as a student, you probably experienced moments of anxiety when you received your report cards. As a teacher, you are responsible for summarizing a student's achievement and efforts into one 'neat' single grade. Whether the grade is an 'A' or a '1,' compressed alpha or numeric values cannot adequately describe the complete nature of a student's learning experience or academic performance. Regardless of individual viewpoints on grading systems, the reality is that compressed reporting systems will not soon disappear. As a teacher you must consider how you plan to collect and document multiple forms of information about a student's progress.

■ How does a teacher determine which assessments to include in averaging work for a report card grade?

It is critical that the teacher makes pre-determined decisions about which formative and summative assessments should be recorded for a fair representation of student achievement over time. For example, a teacher may decide to weight formative assessments at 60 percent and summative assessments at 40 percent of a quarter's grade.

■ Does a teacher need to include all assessments in averaging grades for end of quarter or semester reporting?

■ © 2008 Jupiter Images Corporation.

Student work should be honored. A teacher must make professional judgments about what assessments reflect a fair judgment of student learning. For example, if the majority of a class does not perform well on a particular assignment or test, the teacher must decide to use that assessment as an indication for the need to reteach content and reevaluate. Students should not be penalized. The key for you as a teacher is to assess and reflect.

The first step to collecting and documenting information about a student's progress is determining what data needs to be collected. Veteran teachers suggest the best place to start is the school's grade-level report card. It is important to note that at the elementary level there are often three types of progress indicators: Effort, Achievement, and Grade Level. In the following reading report card, teachers assess student progress for all three "grades" for this subject.

The following case study reviews Ms. Reed's actions as she determined how she would collect information about each student and how she would quantify this information for the report card.

READING SECTION OF A REPORT CARD

Student _____ Date _____

Progress Indicators

Academic Achievement	**Effort**	**Grade Level**
1=Outstanding	E=Excels	B=Beyond Level
2=Very Good	S=Satisfactory	G=Grade Level
3=Satisfactory	N=Needs Improvement	L=Below Level
4=Having Difficulty		
5=Having Serious Difficulty		

Reading	1st Quarter	2nd Quarter	3rd Quarter	4th Quarter
Fluency				
Oral				
Comprehension				
Vocabulary				
Independent Reading				
Academic Achievement:				
Effort:				
Grade Level:				

Ms. Reed reviewed the reading curriculum guide and report card with the grade-level team. After the team had established a long-term curriculum plan for reading, Ms. Reed began to collect information about her students. In addition to their reading levels, Ms. Reed wanted to know how her students felt about themselves as readers, and what each student liked to read. Since the report card required information about grade level, reading fluency, comprehension, and effort, she knew she would need to collect information that reflected these skills.

Ms. Reed used checklists, observation notes, placement tests, and running records to collect relevant reading data for all of her students. Each week she would review and quantify (grade) the students' products and efforts. Initially this was a time-consuming process. To help save time, Ms. Reed created a scoring equivalency chart.

Sample Grading Scales

Outstanding = O	93–100	A	1	Excellent
	90–93	A–	1–	
	87–89	B+	2+	
Satisfactory = S	83–86	B	2	Above Average
	80–82	B–	2–	
	77–79	C+	3+	
	73–76	C	3	Average
	70–72	C–	3–	
Needs Improvement = N	67–69	D+	4+	Below Average
	63–66	D	4	
	60–62	D–	4–	
Failing = F	59	F	5	Failing

GRADE LEVEL

Tom Reynolds is reading beyond grade-level. The teacher, Ms. Reed, determined his reading level by using two ongoing assessment measures: a Running Record and a Reading Inventory. Both of these measures offer diagnostic and placement information about Tom's reading performance. The following page presents his reading grades.

READING ACHIEVEMENT

Ms. Reed determined Tom's reading achievement grades by combining the grades they received on oral reading fluency and comprehension. Oral reading fluency was assessed through the individualized running records Ms. Reed took once every other week. In case she may need to review, Ms. Reed audiotaped each running record for each student. Each student had a tape cassette labelled and stored in their reading folder. To obtain the comprehension grade, Ms. Reed once again relied upon the running record. After each reading, Ms. Reed asked the students to retell the story. She also asked "prompt" questions that stimulated inferential responses. Ms. Reed used a "Story Retelling Checklist" to guide her assessments. Tom read fluently and was able to comprehend even the most complex plots.

EFFORT GRADE

Tom's effort grade was determined by several factors. First, Ms. Reed asked the students to read their assigned pages for Reader's Workshop and respond in their journal at least once each week. Second, Ms. Reed observed student interactions with literature during DEAR (Drop Everything And Read). She recorded and dated these observations. Tom showed satisfactory effort. Occasionally he forgot to read and reflect upon the assigned pages for Reader's Workshop. Several times during DEAR he distracted others.

Sample Reading Section of a Report Card

Student Tom Reynolds _____ Date October 16th _____

Progress Indicators

Academic Achievement	**Effort**	**Grade Level**
1 = Outstanding	E = Excels	B = Beyond Level
2 = Very Good	S = Satisfactory	G = Grade Level
3 = Satisfactory	N = Needs Improvement	L = Below Level
4 = Having Difficulty		
5 = Having Serious Difficulty		

Reading	1st Quarter	2nd Quarter	3rd Quarter	4th Quarter
Fluency	1			
Oral	1			
Comprehension	2			
Vocabulary	1			
Independent Reading	3			
Academic Achievement:	1			
Effort:	S			
Grade Level:	B			

Portfolios

SELECTING STUDENT WORK

Ms. Reed had a working folder for each of her students. It contained all their tests and the work for which Ms. Reed had recorded grades. From the working folder, Ms. Reed selected the samples that would represent the typical range of each student's work, as well as the student's best work. This work is then organized in a performance or showcase portfolio.

PORTFOLIO EVALUATION SYSTEM

After Ms. Reed selected relevant work to include in the student portfolio, she:

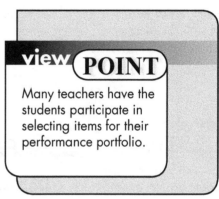

viewPOINT

Many teachers have the students participate in selecting items for their performance portfolio.

- Used a sturdy two-pocket folder with center tabs that helped to organize observational notes in a sequential manner.
- Labeled the portfolio with the student's name and number.
- Filed all the formal evaluations that she has given, such as standardized test results, unit tests, district criterion-referenced tests, and placement tests.
- Filed all informal tests (these could include reading inventories, running records and teacher-made tests).
- Collected and filed all the samples she had of work from all content areas.

In addition to test score results and grades, the portfolio allows Ms. Reed an opportunity to document each student's development over time.

Barootchi and Keshavarz' study determined that portfolio assessment contributed to English as a Foreign Language (EFL) learners' academic achievement and their feeling of responsibility towards monitoring their progress. The portfolio assessment scores correlated significantly with those of the teacher-made achievement test, and high inter-rater reliability was also achieved. Therefore it is concluded that portfolio assessment, as a promising testing and teaching tool for teachers in EFL classes, can be used in conjunction with teacher-made tests to provide the continuous, ongoing measurement of student growth needed for formative evaluation and for planning instructional programs.

Barootchi, N., & Keshavarz, M.H. (2002). Assessment of achievement through portfolios and teacher-made tests. *Educational Research, 44*(3), 279–288.

evaluation QUESTIONS

- How will you document student growth and development?

- How will you report student learning?

Questions for Reflection

DOCUMENTING STUDENT GROWTH

- How will you manage student grades?
- How will you use anecdotal notes?
- How will you collect data?
- How will you determine what to assess?

REPORTING STUDENT LEARNING

- How will you explain the school's report card to a parent?
- How will you communicate progress to students?
- How will you motivate students for ongoing learning through specific feedback?

Self-Assessment of Professional Growth

Name				Date	
Grade Level/Content Area					

Measures for Assessment	Low				High
To what degree do I have the knowledge needed to effectively use varying measures to assess student learning?	1 ☐	2 ☐	3 ☐	4 ☐	5 ☐
To what degree do I have the skills needed to effectively use varying measures to assess student learning?	1 ☐	2 ☐	3 ☐	4 ☐	5 ☐
On-Demand and Ongoing Assessments	Low				High
To what degree do I have the knowledge needed to effectively use on-demand and ongoing assessment to guide instruction?	1 ☐	2 ☐	3 ☐	4 ☐	5 ☐
To what degree do I have the skills needed to effectively use the teaching standards in my practice?	1 ☐	2 ☐	3 ☐	4 ☐	5 ☐
Documenting Student Growth	Low				High
To what degree do I have the knowledge needed to document student growth and development?	1 ☐	2 ☐	3 ☐	4 ☐	5 ☐
To what degree do I have the skills needed to document student growth and development?	1 ☐	2 ☐	3 ☐	4 ☐	5 ☐
Reporting Student Learning	Low				High
To what degree do I have the knowledge needed to report student learning and development?	1 ☐	2 ☐	3 ☐	4 ☐	5 ☐
To what degree do I have the skills needed to report student learning and development?	1 ☐	2 ☐	3 ☐	4 ☐	5 ☐

Set goals for next steps to implement best practices in the teaching standard of assessment.

_____

_____

_____

_____

_____

_____

_____

_____

_____

_____

_____

_____

_____

_____

_____

_____

_____

_____

Collaboration: Managing Communications

⑤

> **❝**To create a professional learning community, focus on learning rather than teaching, work collaboratively, and hold yourself accountable for results.**❞**
>
> —RICHARD DUFOUR

An important aspect of building community is establishing positive rapport with parents. One of a teacher's most important tasks is to communicate with the parents about their students. Research consistently reveals that when parents are involved in their son or daughter's education, the student, of any age, benefits. Teachers who effectively and frequently communicate with parents increase the chances that parents will:

- become meaningfully involved in their son/daughter's education
- reinforce classroom instruction
- support the teacher's management system.

POINTS OF INQUIRY

- How will you design your classroom Back to School Night and Open House to initiate positive working relationships?
- What will you implement to sustain ongoing communications with parents to benefit student achievement?
- In what ways will you establish and maintain collegial collaborations?
- How will you design a system of support to accommodate the diverse needs of your students?

Parent Interactions

> " When teachers show they care enough to communicate with parents about their child, they gain an ally in helping the child be a success. "

—MATT BROWN

Welcoming Classroom Events

Most schools host one or two events at the onset of the school year to acquaint the students and parents with the teacher, classroom, and curriculum. Typically the Back to School event is held before the first day of school, and includes parents and students. Within the first month after the students have been attending, the Open House takes place and is usually designed for parent attendance. Check with your school and district for specifics related to these events.

BACK TO SCHOOL

Some schools conduct a "Meet the Teacher" or "Back to School" event just prior to the opening of school.

You may want to distribute a Back-to-School Kit, which includes:

- the school newsletter;
- information about the parent-teacher organization;
- a list of supplies needed for school;
- the class schedule;
- a school map;
- the lunch menu for the month;
- a form that provides parents' home and work information;
- an emergency form;
- a "Getting to Know Your Child" questionnaire;
- a volunteer card.

view POINT

Students will enter your classroom throughout the year. To assist their families in adjusting to a new school, make extra Back-to-School Kits.

ROOM ROAM

Allow students and parents time to orient themselves with the classroom. The Room Roam activity can help provide guidelines. Be available for questions and introduce yourself to each student and parent. Use this time to begin your positive interactions.

Sample Back to School Activity

Room Roam

1. Find your desk. It has your name on it.

2. Make name tags for you and your parents.

3. Find the fish tank. Count the number of fish in the fish tank.

4. Find the Birthday Chart. When is your birthday? Write it on the Birthday Chart.

5. Find the Tooth Graph. How many teeth have you lost? Put that number on the Tooth Graph.

6. Find the "Me" bulletin board. Draw your portrait and write your name on it. Then put it on the "Me" bulletin board.

7. Find the information desk. Have your parents complete the information forms in the Back-to-School Kit.

8. Make a new friend.

OPEN HOUSE

Successful Open Houses allow you to inform parents about the learning activities the students are experiencing and describe the instructional program. It is also an opportunity to expand your knowledge of the students and their parents. Typically, the parents attend an assembly for school-wide information and then attend a 15–20 minute orientation in their son's or daughter's class. This allows parents an opportunity to "get a feel for" their child's class and their teacher.

To encourage attendance, it is important to formally invite parents early, and remind them of the day and time.

You may want to hold a competition between your classes or grade level competing for the most parents attending. The winning class receives a pizza party, a free period on Friday or a "one-time-only" homework pass.

Listed below are several activities that can be organized for Open House. Implement your choices based on grade level and content area.

Teacher Greeting Wear a name tag and greet parents at the door. Highlight something about each student as they come in. Introduce yourself to the parents you haven't met before.

Mentor Voices

➤ "Introduce yourself to parents and establish a relationship before challenges develop."

Open House Invitation

ANYTOWN SCHOOL

Welcomes Your Family
to
Open House
Tuesday, September 12
7:00 PM

Student Entertainment, Door Prizes, Refreshments
See You There!

▬ Sample Open House Invitation

Parent Notes and Name Tags All students make their parents' name tags. Have students write a welcome note to their parents or have a work sample on their desks or tables.

Teacher Presentation This presentation should be brief and positive. Address issues such as daily schedules, classroom rules and expectations, learning centers, homework assignments, and special activities. Remember to dress professionally, and smile.

Handouts Provide a handout that summarizes the content of the presentation. Remember, the handout may need to be translated into other languages. This can also be given to parents who may have been unable to attend.

Student Demonstrations If your school encourages student attendance, you can have students engage in group songs, choral readings, or curriculum overviews. They can create these themselves as a class assignment, or the presentation can be something you have chosen for them. Knowing that their child has a specific role may encourage more parents to come.

Reviewing Teaching Approach There are many approaches to teaching. Parents appreciate knowing how and what their children will be taught this year in your classroom. Highlight your grade level curriculum guide, student standards, and your instructional strategies.

Contact Form Open House is a night to meet and welcome all families. Unfortunately, some parents may try to monopolize your time to deal with more personal issues. If parents try to engage you in an individual conference, you can firmly and politely redirect them by offering a contact form to complete.

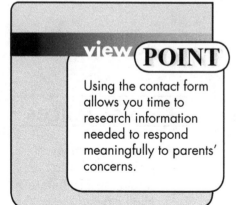

view POINT

Using the contact form allows you time to research information needed to respond meaningfully to parents' concerns.

CONTACT FORM

Student Name_____ Parent Name/s _____

Home Phone _____ Work Phone _____

Cell Phone _____ E-mail _____

Please contact for a meeting time.   By phone _____   In person _____

Best times for contact:_____

Topics to discuss:_____

_____

_____

_____

_____

_____

_____

_____

_____

_____

_____

_____

_____

_____

_____

■ Sample Quilt

School/Class Policies Check with front office for any universal message that the administration and/or department may want on the board for all parents to read, such as the tardy policy. You may also want to distribute the school or class handbook, identifying school-wide policies or classroom expectations.

Class Quilt Students and the teacher draw and label pictures of themselves. Arrange pictures in a quilt-like fashion. This creates a strong sense of classroom community and can be showcased at Open House.

Refreshments Serve light refreshments. Ask for parent contributions or request funding from the parent organization.

Door Prizes Hold drawings for door prizes, such as children's books, markers, fancy pencils, or items with the school logo. Teachers can encourage parents to complete an information card and drop it in a fish bowl. The teacher draws one or two cards per class and gives away items.

PARENT VOLUNTEERS

Many parents and grandparents look forward to volunteering in their child's classroom, or even are available to help from home. Distribute volunteer cards to know which types of activities parents would be willing to assist with. Cards can also be used for drawing door prizes at Back to School or Open House.

Volunteer Options

Celebration Planners Help by planning and managing classroom celebrations throughout the year. One parent may wish to take the lead for each party. These parents and grandparents usually make a two- to three-hour time commitment about four times a year.

Parent Tutors Work with students in small groups, or tutor one-to-one. This type of parental role requires parents who are willing to make consistent weekly commitments. These parents and grandparents should be willing to spend time planning and debriefing with the teachers.

view POINT

Whatever parent jobs you decide on, be sure to help parents and grandparents complete their tasks successfully the first time. For example, it will be necessary to demonstrate how to use the copier, work the laminator, or place a book order.

Parent Helpers Help classroom through options such as preparing learning activities or creating bulletin boards. These parents and grandparents should make monthly or bimonthly time commitments.

At-Home Helpers Support classroom teacher through options such as preparing games, creating bulletin boards, or organizing and managing book orders. These parents and grandparents need to respond to time deadlines, but may work at home to complete tasks.

Field Trip Helpers Accompany students and teachers on field trips. Help manage student behavior and assist teacher.

ORGANIZING VOLUNTEERS

Keeping track of your parent help requires a little organization. After you have collected your parent volunteer forms, condense the information for your easy reference and keep it easily accessible to contact parents when a volunteer activity is needed.

view POINT

Research has consistently demonstrated that parent involvement is positively correlated to student achievement. The teacher's role should be to encourage and manage parental participation in many ways.

GUIDELINES FOR PARENT VOLUNTEERS

Once you have determined what capacity parents or grandparents are interested in, it is time to conduct "Job Alike" workshops. If you have two or three parents who wish to be "Parent Helpers" or "At-Home Parent Helpers," ask them to meet with you for a time period after school. At this time you can review the specifics of certain tasks you will be asking them to complete.

Beyond sharing the "how-to-do-its," it is also time to review school policies and discuss any questions they might have.

- Do they need to sign in at the office?
- Do they need to wear name tags?
- Where do they park?
- Can they bring younger children?

view POINT

It is important to remind parents about maintaining students' confidentiality.

VOLUNTEER CARD

Parent Name/s _____

Student's Name _____

Home Phone _____   Work Phone _____

Cell Phone _____   E-mail _____

I would be willing to:

_____ Coordinate classroom celebrations

_____ Work in classroom with students

_____ Work in classroom on assigned tasks

_____ Work at home on assigned tasks

_____ Other _____

Please list any other ways you would be willing to assist our class.

_____

_____

_____

_____

_____

_____

_____

_____

_____

_____

_____

_____

Sample Volunteer Organization Chart

Parent Helper	Phone #	Parent Helper	At-Home Helper	Celebration Planner	Parent Tutor	Notes
Mrs. Smith	(602) 555-6210				✓ M*	Fall Curriculum
Mr. Turner	(602) 555-8355	✓ T* 11:00				Likes to do graphics and science
Mrs. Valdez	(602) 555-4385	✓				Computer tech
Mrs. Marks	(602) 555-6153			✓		Art appreciation
Mrs. Pratz	(602) 555-7865	✓ T*		✓ F*		Field trip sponsor
Mrs. Jones	(602) 555-2386		✓			Speaker

* Denotes day parents are available to work

Ongoing Contacts

Communicating with parents can be done most effectively if done proactively. Classroom publications should be designed to review student learning activities or directly inform parents about specific concepts.

◼◼ © 2008 Jupiter Images Corporation.

NEWSLETTERS

Newsletters can be an effective home-school communication tool. When sent out regularly, parents will begin to expect them and what type of information they provide. Be sure to represent yourself professionally by sending out an error-free newsletter with an appealing format. Your written communications will make a lasting impression. Have a colleague or your mentor edit your work for grammar, spelling, and, most importantly, a positive "tone." For example, "Students need to wear comfortable clothes to school," not "Students should not wear dress clothes to school."

First-Day Communiqué During the opening day of school you have a perfect opportunity to introduce yourself, establish expectations and routine procedures, and ask for parental support. The first-day communiqué to the parents should introduce you as the teacher, describe some feature of the learning activities the students will experience in your class, review classroom expectations, and encourage parents to contact you if they have questions. Your communiqué might refer to the school newsletter or handbook, which often includes information about school hours, bus schedules, attendance policies and procedures, and cafeteria information. It can also introduce features of upcoming weekly newsletters.

Parent Perspective Questionnaires can provide valuable information that will help you meet your students' needs. This survey could be sent home with the student on the first day of school or completed at Back to School or Open House.

© Jaimie Duplass 2008. Under license from Shutterstock, Inc.

Sample Parent Questionnaire

I am looking forward to being your child's teacher. Since your child's learning, happiness and health are so important to me, I am asking you to answer the following questions and return. I look forward to getting to know both you and your child better.

Name Jennifer Vandush   Age 6 Date of Birth 1/21

Parent/Guardian Name/s Claudia and John Vandush

Home Phone (480)555-4287   Work Phone (480)555-5376

E-mail JVandush@email.org

1. How will your child be transported to and from school? School bus

2. How is your child's overall health? Good, but she does have asthma.

3. Are there health concerns that I should know about? Food allergies? Colds? Ear infections? No

4. List any medications your child takes regularly. Inhaler as needed.

5. How many hours of sleep a night does your child usually get? 9 hours

6. List the names and ages of your other children.

    Brian 7 years old

    Amanda 3 years old

7. What activities does your child enjoy the most? Jennifer enjoys sports. She likes computer

    games and playing with her friends.

8. What languages are spoken in the home? English

9. What are you child's favorite TV shows? Movies? Sailor Moon /Dr. Doolittle

10. What is the title of your child's favorite book? I Spy

11. Are there other concerns or things that I should know about? No

PARENT QUESTIONNAIRE

I am looking forward to being your child's teacher. Since your child's learning, happiness and health are so important to me, I am asking you to answer the following questions and return. I look forward to getting to know both you and your child better.

Name _____ Age _____ Date of Birth _____

Parent/Guardian Name/s _____

Home Phone _____ Work Phone _____

E-mail _____

1. How will your child be transported to and from school? _____

2. How is your child's overall health? _____

3. Are there health concerns that I should know about? Food allergies? Colds? Ear infections? ____
    _____

4. List any medications your child takes regularly. _____

5. How many hours of sleep a night does your child usually get? _____

6. List the names and ages of your other children. _____
    _____
    _____

7. What activities does your child enjoy the most? _____
    _____
    _____

8. What languages are spoken in the home? _____

9. What are you child's favorite TV shows? Movies? _____

10. What is the title of your child's favorite book? _____

11. Are there other concerns or things that I should know about? _____
    _____

Weekly Newsletters One-page newsletters need to be sent weekly. They should:

- be reader-friendly and conversational;
- review briefly the high points of student learning;
- preview the goals and activities planned for the coming week;
- recognize parents who have helped support classroom learning; for example, parents who accompanied the class on a field trip;
- provide announcements;
- be sent home consistently on one particular day of the week; Mondays are generally best;
- have consistent sections each week so parents know where to look for specific information.

The following page offers an example of a weekly newsletter, and includes easy-to-read and relevant classroom information.

Monthly Newsletters By third grade, students can begin to write regular columns in newsletters. Monthly newsletters created with teacher and student input enhance a sense of community. They provide parents with an opportunity to preview the curriculum and classroom projects for the upcoming month, and review recent learning. Monthly newsletters are generally two to three pages in length. They can include features such as: From a Kid's Eye View, Dear Teacher, Monthly Calendar, and Curriculum Overview to inform parents in a fun and interesting manner.

Teachers can involve students in the following way:

1. The teacher assigns groups of students to cover featured sections of the monthly newsletter.

2. Students gather resources needed.

3. Writing teams write and peer edit each other's work.

4. The teacher provides feedback and assists for computer input, formatting, and final editing.

view POINT

English may not be the parents' first language. Therefore, a teacher should attempt to have all written communication translated into the language appropriate for the student's parents.

view POINT

When you send home newsletters, be sure to file in a section of your teacher notebook or lesson plan book. This practice provides you a complete and immediate record of correspondence, and provides easy access for coordinating curriculum with parent communication for the following year.

© 2008 Jupiter Images Corporation.

Sample Weekly Newsletter

ALONE WE CAN DO SO LITTLE, TOGETHER WE CAN DO SO MUCH. -HELEN KELLER

Schoolhouse of Honea

VOLUME 1, ISSUE 4   SEPTEMBER 23

DATES TO REMEMBER:

- **September 23:** Open House from 6:00PM to 8:00PM

- **September 27:** State Capitol Field Trip

- **September 30:** Early Release at 12:30PM

WORDS OF WISDOM:

Every day, an old man walked up the beach with a pail, picking up starfish that had been washed in by the tide and throwing them back into the sea. One day a young boy stopped the old man and asked, "Why do you throw the starfish back? It doesn't matter. They will only wash up on the shore again tomorrow."

The old man picked a starfish out of his pail, threw it as far as he could into the sea, and replied...

"It mattered to that one."

- Author Unknown

A Week at a Glance

This past week the students have participated in various learning activities.

Math: We reviewed multiplication and division facts 1 through 12. The students are really understanding the concept and ready to move to the next step.

Reading: Students read from two different cultural versions of *Little Red Riding Hood* and compared multiple aspects of the story. We also began reading *Esperanza Rising* during teacher read-aloud time.

Science: We began an introductory unit on the planets and students began researching a planet of their choice.

Social Studies: We are coming to a close on the judicial system unit. This week students engaged in a mock Senate session. Thanks to the parents who assisted in the organization of this great learning experience.

A Look to the Future

This week's learning opportunities include many new concepts and ideas.

Math: We will continue practicing multiplication and division, as well as begin learning how to multiply double-digits.

Reading: In our reading textbook, we will be reading and comparing two cultural versions of Cinderella. We will continue reading *Esperanza Rising* during teacher read-aloud.

Science: Students will continue researching their planet and then sharing their knowledge. They will begin making a plan for their solar system diagrams.

Social Studies: We will be taking a field trip to the State Capitol this week as culmination to the judicial system unit.

People to Know

Classroom
Teacher: Ms. J. Honea Rm 13
Direct Line: 480-555-0013
Email: jhonea@school.org

Teacher's Aide: Ms. L. Andrew

ELL Aide: Ms. S. Martin

Resource Teacher:
Ms. H. Smith

School Office
Principal: Mrs. B. Haily

Office Assistant: Ms. J. Higgins
Direct Line: 480-555-0000

Nurse: Mrs. N. Hall
Direct Line: 480-555-0072

Attendance Line:
480-555-0071

District Office
Superintendent: Dr. J. Weiss

Asst. Superintendents:
Mrs. G. Layen
Mr. H. Johan
Dr. L. Batey

Office Assistant: Mrs. R. Coop
Direct Line: 480-555-6613

Classroom Wish List

✓ Styrofoam balls (various sizes)
✓ Metal hangers
✓ Elmer's glue
✓ Tempera paint
✓ Boxes of tissues
✓ Hand sanitizer

Thanks to Mrs. Hardy for supplying snacks this week and next week. The students and I greatly appreciate them.

Announcements

☆ Open House is tonight from 6-8. Come visit our classroom to see what your child has been learning.

☆ Our *Star Student of the Week* is Joseph Gall. He is a hard worker and a good friend to classmates.

☆ I will be out on Monday and Tuesday of next week to attend a professional training on implementing our new reading program.

Newsletter created by Joanna Honea

This activity has several positive features:

- It serves as a closure-summarization activity.
- Students have an opportunity to practice writing a brief, journalistic text.
- Students work together to edit and improve their own and others' writing skills.
- Each student in the classroom is co-author of two articles.
- Parents receive frequent communication about classroom activities from students' perspective.
- Students have a regular and authentic opportunity to publish their work for others to read and appreciate.

News Flashes There are times when events occur or announcements must be shared that require immediate publication. News Flashes are very brief, but still cover the Who, What, Where, When, and Why.

News Flash

Our Science Fair last night was a huge success! News Channel 3 came out and will be airing a piece tonight during the 6:00PM and 10:00PM newscasts. The piece will include interviews with multiple parents and our very own students. Congratulations to all 5th and 6th graders for their inquiry and hard work in making the Science Fair a success.

■ Sample News Flash

PHONE/E-MAIL LOGS

Personal interactions are opportunities for parents and teachers to share information about a student's needs in two-way verbal or written communication. A powerful tool for communicating with parents is the telephone. Unfortunately, phone calls have traditionally been reserved for "bad news." Whenever possible, however, the phone should be used as an instrument of good news. Successful teachers have found that brief, positive, frequent telephone conversations help to establish strong partnerships with parents. When parents receive a phone call regarding something positive, they immediately sense the teacher's enthusiasm for teaching their son/daughter and are more likely to become involved in classroom activities and support the teacher.

In today's technological society, e-mails are often a preferred method of communication. Remember, however, that your tone is sometimes lost within written communication, so re-read what you have written to make sure it reflects your message. In addition, many schools and individual classroom teachers maintain websites for ongoing and up-to-date information and communication. All correspondence to parents should be documented. The example below shows ways to manage and maintain records of phone conversations. E-mails can be printed and filed in the student's parent communication file or stored in an on-line folder.

Sample Phone Call Log

Student Name _Robert Romero_____ Parent Name/s _Mrs. Rodriquez_____

Phone __555-7272_____

Date _Feb. 2nd_____ Regarding _Student has been absent for 3 days_____

Action _Robert has chicken pox; he will be out at least 4 more days. Older brother will_

_pick up get well card from class and deliver work._____

_____

_____

Date _March 3rd_____ Regarding _Academic progress_____

Action _Robert is having great success with reading, especially in paired reading. Is_

hesitant to write during writer's workshop. Teacher will send home writing briefcase

_and have parents write a story with Robert._____

_____

Date _April 12th_____ Regarding _Writing progress_____

Action __Robert is showing more comfort and confidence with his writing. He shared a_

_story he wrote with his parents to the class today._____

_____

_____

PHONE CALL LOG

Student Name _____   Parent Name/s _____

Phone _____

Date _____   Regarding _____

Action _____

_____

_____

_____

_____

Date _____   Regarding _____

Action _____

_____

_____

_____

_____

Date _____   Regarding _____

Action _____

_____

_____

_____

_____

Date _____   Regarding _____

Action _____

_____

_____

_____

view POINT

Conferences are physically, intellectually, and emotionally demanding. You may wish to bring nutritious snacks and beverages to sustain your energy.

CONFERENCES

Successful conferences are the result of careful planning and organization. A successful conference means that parents and teachers have:

- shared information about the student and both have a better understanding and appreciation of the student's needs and abilities.
- developed a mutual trust and respect for each other and will continue to work together for the benefit of the student.

Conference Planning and Scheduling Begin scheduling conferences at least two weeks prior to the first conference dates. To do this, you will need to make sure that you:

- arrange conferences so parents can attend early in the morning, after school or in the evening;
- allow 15–20 minutes per conference and schedule at least five minutes between conferences;
- establish a first-response, first-scheduled policy;
- allow a choice of three time slots in order of preference so that parents may schedule conferences at convenient times. Parents are more likely to attend if they have a choice of time;
- include a response confirmation sheet.

When a majority of parents have returned their request, phone the parents who have not responded (this saves a great deal of frustration and "paper tag"). After you have scheduled everyone, publish a confirmed schedule listing all appointments; this reminds parents and reaffirms the importance of everyone's participation. A sample scheduling letter is provided on the following page.

Preparing for Progress Review Conference Students of all ages are highly complex, social individuals who must function appropriately in two different worlds: school and home. Parents need to understand how a student uses his/her social skills to become a productive member in the classroom community. Likewise, teachers need to understand the student's home life and recognize its significant influence on a student's behavior, interests, and ability to learn.

Parent/teacher communications reach their full potential when parents and teachers share information about the student from their unique perspectives, value the student's individual strengths and needs, and work together for the benefit of the student. The best opportunity teachers have for engaging parents in this interaction is during the parent/teacher conference. Conferences, which feature a positive two-way exchange, are the result of careful planning and organization. There are generally two types of parent/teacher conferences, the pre-established conference that reviews the student's classroom progress, and spontaneous conferences that deal with a range of specific concerns that occur throughout the school year.

The Progress Review Conference is an opportunity for both partners to share information about the student's social interactions, emotional maturity, and cognitive development in school and at home. One way to help a parent prepare to be an active member during the conference is a pre-conference questionnaire. The parent questionnaire also gives the teacher a preview of parent concerns. This allows the teacher time to collect information to be better prepared for the conference. The chart on page 200 provides a format for a pre-conference questionnaire.

Sample Scheduling Letter

Hello,

I am looking forward to talking with each of you during Parent/Teacher Conference Week, November 1–5. Please sign up for the three time slots that are most convenient for you. To assure you receive the time slot that is best for you, please send in the response form as soon as possible.

Please note that, because of parent-teacher conferences, students will be released at 12:00 PM. on Thursday, November 4th and all day Friday, November 5th.

Student's Name _____ Teacher _____

Parent's Name _____ Phone _____

Place a 1, 2 and 3 by your first three choices of conference times.

Tuesday AM	**Wednesday AM**	**Thursday PM**	**Friday AM**
7:40 _____	7:40 _____	2:00 _____	7:40 _____
8:00 _____	8:00 _____	2:20 _____	8:00 _____
		2:40 _____	8:20 _____
		3:00 _____	8:40 _____
		3:20 _____	9:00 _____
		3:40 _____	9:20 _____
		BREAK	BREAK
		4:20 _____	10:00 _____
		4:40 _____	10:20 _____
		5:00 _____	10:40 _____
		5:20 _____	11:00 _____
		5:40 _____	11:20 _____
		6:00 _____	11:40 _____
		6:20 _____	BREAK
		6:40 _____	1:00 _____
			1:20 _____
			1:40 _____
			2:00 _____
			2:20 _____
			2:40 _____
			BREAK
			3:20 _____
			3:40 _____
			4:00 _____
			4:20 _____
			4:40 _____

Greetings,

To help us make the most of our parent/teacher time, I am sending this questionnaire to help facilitate our progress review conference. Please read and complete the questions. If you have any other concerns, list them on the questionnaire and we will discuss any of your inquiries during our time together. Please return by: _____.

Child's Name _____

Parent/Guardian Completing Form _____

1. How would you describe your son/daughter's attitude towards school?

2. What school activity does your son/daughter most enjoy?

3. What school activity does your son/daughter least enjoy?

4. How do you think you can help your son/daughter learn?

5. Are there any unique situations or challenges you want to share to help me understand your son/daughter better?

Thank you for your help.

Sincerely,

(Teacher Name)

Sharing Student Progress During the Progress Review Conference the teacher will, of course, share information about the student's academic progress. Beyond test scores, portfolio artifacts, and academic progress, however, most parents also want to know about their son/daughter's social interactions and classroom behavior.

To keep the conference focused and allow time to review all aspects of the student's performance in 15 minutes, it is important to use a structured format during the progress review conference. The structure increases the chance that both the teacher and parent concerns are adequately discussed.

Four-Step Conference Plan Following a conference plan will allow for a more productive and focused conference. In some cases, depending on who initiates the conference, parent or teacher, the order of input may be reversed, or be more of a fluid interchange of questions and responses.

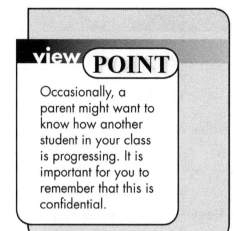

view POINT

Occasionally, a parent might want to know how another student in your class is progressing. It is important for you to remember that this is confidential.

1. *Opening*—The teacher's opening statements help establish a foundation for a proactive conference. Use this time to identify conference objectives and set a positive tone. Positive statements need to be sincere. For example, "Lydia is eager to learn."

2. *Parent Input*—"First, I am going to ask you to share with me what you have observed about Lydia this year that makes you feel good about her learning, and also what questions or concerns you have about her progress."

(It is important for parents to focus on their son/daughter's academic and social strengths when they meet with you. It is also important for you to know what the parents view as their son/daughter's major academic or social concerns.)

3. *Teacher Input*—"Now, I will share some of Lydia's work with you and my observations about her progress. We'll discuss ideas that will continue to encourage her learning."

(The success of the parent/teacher relationship depends upon the teacher's ability to highlight the student's academic/social strengths and progress. When areas of concern are discussed, it is important to provide examples of the student's work or to review the observational data to illustrate the point. Often the issues the parents reveal are directly related to the teacher's concerns. Whenever possible, connect these concerns. This reinforces the feeling that the teacher and the parents have the same goals for helping the student grow. It is essential to solicit the parents' views and suggestions for helping the child, and also provide concrete examples to help the student improve.)

4. *Closure*—"Finally, we'll summarize the conference by reviewing the home and school activities that will best help Lydia continue to progress."

(To make sure both teacher and parents have reached a common understanding, it is necessary to briefly review the main ideas and suggestions for action that were discussed during the conference.)

CONFERENCE PLANNER

Student Name_____ Parent Name/s _____

Conference Date _____ Time _____

Other Teachers Present _____

1. Welcome and Positive Statement _____

Review Conference Steps—After I review our conference objectives, I will ask you to review _____ progress, sharing with me both academic/social strengths and areas of concern. Next, I'll review work with you and discuss academic/social strengths and areas in which we will want _____ to grow. Finally, we will discuss the main points we discussed today and review the strategies that will help _____ make progress.

2. Parent Input—What have you observed about _____ this year that makes you feel good about his/her learning?

_____

_____

_____

What are your main concerns? _____

_____

3. Teacher Input—I would like to share some observations about _____ work and review the areas of strengths and the skills that need to be refined.

_____

_____

_____

4. Closure—Let's review the things we talked about that will facilitate continued success.

_____

_____

_____

STUDENT – PARENT – TEACHER CONFERENCES

Another innovation in conferences is the inclusion of the students. The students participate equally; sharing their work, discussing areas that he/she has noticed improvement, and establishing academic and/or social goals. This type of conference requires the student to be an active participant in selecting what work will be featured in the portfolio. In addition, the teacher must help students develop the skill to evaluate their own performance.

Since a three-way conference may be a new experience for parents, it is important for the teacher to establish guidelines for parents and students. A letter sent home explaining the format of the conference and discussing each person's role is essential. Parents are encouraged to ask open-ended questions, such as:

- "What did you learn about the most?"
- "What did you work the hardest to learn?"
- "What do you want to learn about more?"

Questions such as these encourage students to analyze their own learning, and also help them to set new goals. Parents should not criticize the child's work or focus on any negative aspect of any material that is presented during the conference. Negative comments, particularly from parents, will only inhibit learning and dampen excitement about school.

 Classroom Scenario

The following is a brief excerpt of a three-way conference at the last conference of the year. Notice that Manuel does most of the talking:

Mother: Manuel, what have you worked hardest to learn?

Manuel: My writing. I can do it faster and all of my friends like reading my stories now. I draw really good illustrations—everybody likes them.

Teacher: Manuel, can you read your parents an excerpt from a favorite story you wrote?

(Manuel reads the pre-determined portion of his story with great confidence. He reads with great fluency and intonation. His parents smile, and are impressed with their son's comical pictures.)

Teacher: Manuel, what else have you been working on?

Manuel: My math facts. I know them all and even helped Shelly and Robbie put together the math facts board.

Father: Manuel, what do you want to learn next year?

Manuel: I want to read more chapter books. I want to get my own library card. I want to learn more math facts, you know, like Maria (his older sister) can do. I want to write more books and publish them in the school library.

Setting the Scene The day of conferences has arrived. You have scheduled parents and have organized the student portfolios, completed report cards, and completed conference format forms. To complete your preparation, consider organizing the waiting and conference areas.

view POINT

In your waiting area, include some of the products the students have created, such as group reports, stories, or a classroom photo album.

view POINT

You may need to have a language translator at some conferences; contact district or school office for suggestions.

Waiting Area On the days of the parent/teacher conferences, you will want to consider providing a waiting area for parents, as even the most carefully planned schedule can go awry. Obviously, it is important that your full attention be focused on the parent/s you are currently meeting. Therefore, if possible, the waiting area should be visually and auditorially set apart from the regular classroom.

Conference Setting To encourage positive interaction and promote two-way dialogue, you may consider conducting the conferences at a "neutral" location, such as a table located in a private section of the classroom. Conducting the conference at your desk, with you sitting directly across from the parents, may convey an adversarial message.

Proactive Statements Sometimes the information you must share about a student is difficult for the parents to hear. How you convey this type of information can "make or break" a conference. Negative statements may cause parents to become defensive and stop listening. Parents will more likely continue to listen if the teacher focuses on the positive and takes a proactive stance. For example, "Joe can pass the class if . . ." rather than "Joe will fail the class unless. . . ." The following examples provide a negative statement, samples of more positive ways to express the same points, and examples of supporting details.

Sample Conference Communication

Teacher Concern	Illustration of Negative Statement	Proactive Replacement Statement	Supporting Details
Not completing class work	*He wastes half the morning fooling around.*	*He has so much energy and curiosity that he is sometimes challenged in keeping focused on his work.*	*He talks to his friends and looks to see what others are doing.*
Insecurity	*When something is hard or difficult for him, he won't even try.*	*He is a good worker when he is familiar with the material. He needs to apply the same habits to unfamiliar material.*	*When the work is difficult, he asks to leave the room, tears the paper, or throws his book on the floor.*
Poor social skills	*If he does not like you, you know it. He makes fun of students who are not in his group.*	*He is very perceptive; he can identify with other people's strengths as well as their weaknesses. This gives him an edge that he sometimes uses to tease other students.*	*He knows what makes others uncomfortable and self-conscious (weight, height, braces); he points it out to them (calls them fat, shorty, tinsel teeth).*

Managing Frustrated Parents   Unfortunately, even the most prepared and tactful teacher will at one time or another deal with a frustrated or hostile parent. Generally, these parents are upset because they believe their son/daughter is not being treated fairly or given enough attention. The following scenario illustrates specific types of hostile behavior. The goal in all cases is to diffuse the parent's anger/frustration and begin to develop solutions to improve or resolve the problem. Illustrative examples of what steps you might take to ease the conference to more productive grounds are provided. Teachers can use both verbal and nonverbal communication to respond to the parent's inner feelings by acknowledging the validity of the parent's concerns.

Occasionally a parent is so angry and verbally abusive that the present conference cannot accomplish anything constructive. If several attempts to refocus the conference have failed, the teacher needs to calmly end the conference by acknowledging that the challenges seem to need more resources to support their discussion and that it should benefit all parties to reschedule another time when the principal and/or other resource personnel may join the discussion.

view POINT

It is important for the teacher to recognize that unreasonable hostility may have origins beyond the student's problems at school. Rescheduling the conference allows tempers to cool and time for the teacher to further investigate possible reasons for the parent's aggressive behavior.

Classroom Scenario

> ### Managing Frustrated Parents
>
> **Parent:**   My son's math has not improved since he was placed with you.
>
> (Teacher should ignore direct "attack." Instead, focus attention on the student's problem.)
>
> **Teacher:**   I'm concerned about his math, too. Let's focus on what we think his academic difficulties are and how we can work together to help him.

Problem-Solving Interactions   At the elementary level, the progress review conference is generally scheduled after the first and the third grading periods. However, this is not the only time teachers may need to meet with parents. The following case study illustrates how the teacher and parents worked together to help identify and resolve a specific problem in the home that was creating tension in school life.

Problem-Solving Interactions

Maria—Six-and-a-half-year-old Maria Kelly had started her first grade at Broadway School as a happy young girl. She knew all of the alphabet sounds and symbols and was using invented spelling to write in her journal. Maria attended kindergarten at Broadway School the year before so she had a number of friends both at school and home. Maria smiled easily and enjoyed doing her schoolwork until the middle of October. At this time Maria showed more emotional sensitivity, had difficulty selecting a book and reading during DEAR (Drop Everything And Read), and did very limited writing during Writer's Workshop time. Several days after Maria's behavior suddenly changed, her teacher, Ms. J., called her parents.

Mr. and Mrs. Kelly, Maria's parents, came to school the following day. Ms. J. described the change in Maria's behavior and asked the parents if they had any ideas about what may have caused the change in Maria. They revealed that since the first week of October, Maria's grandmother, who had become widowed that summer, moved into the Kelly's house. Since the grandmother was still grieving, both Mr. and Mrs. Kelly were spending a great deal of time in the evening consoling her. Ms. J. asked if Maria's evening or bedtime routines had been altered since her grandma had moved into the house. After thinking for a moment, both parents admitted they had been spending most of their time either talking to Grandmother or talking to each other about her psychological health and financial situation. Before Grandmother moved in, they had regularly watched TV with their daughter and had an established bedtime routine of storybook reading. They had both noticed that even though they were sending Maria to bed at the same time, they often found her awake when they went to bed a couple of hours later.

At that point in the discussion, it was becoming clear to the Kellys and Ms. J. that at least part of Maria's challenge was related to not getting enough sleep and having a change in her home environment. They reasoned that she might be having difficulty falling asleep because her normal bedtime routines had been disrupted. Mrs. Kelly also felt that Maria, an only child, might be feeling somewhat displaced at home and uncertain of the recent family dynamics.

Ms. J. asked the Kellys what they thought they could do to help Maria deal with her feelings and to adjust to the new situation in their home. Both Mr. and Mrs. Kelly felt they needed to resume Maria's normal bedtime routine immediately. The Kellys wanted Ms. J. to keep them informed of Maria's behavior. Ms. J. suggested that she could send home a personal note with Maria each day for the next two weeks. The Kellys were grateful to Ms. J. for bringing Maria's behavior to their attention. Ms. J. was pleased that the Kellys would be attending to Maria's sleep needs and were very willing to begin to resolve the contextual problems.

best PRACTICES

In a study of 234 ethnically diverse parents of school students, the parents rated the importance of knowing what their children were learning in school and the importance of helping their children with academic work. Drummond and Stipek found that parents rated the importance of involvement in their child's academics higher when a teacher recommended that they help.

In addition, the study indicated that parents perceived the school as a viable source of information. Therefore, teachers need to be committed to communicating with parents about their children's learning.

Drummond, K.V., Stipek, D. (2004, January). Low-income parents' beliefs about their role in children's academic learning. *The Elementary School Journal, 104*(3), 197–213.

Questions for Reflection

evaluation QUESTIONS?

- How will you design your classroom Back to School Night and Open House to initiate positive working relationships?
- What will you implement to sustain ongoing communications with parents to benefit student achievement?

PARENT INTERACTIONS

- How will you plan for Open House or Meet the Teacher?
- How will you encourage parent participation at Open House?
- How will you share information about your teaching philosophy?
- How will you share information about your instructional approach?

ONGOING PARENTAL CONTACTS

- How will you organize and design a plan for ongoing communication with parents?
- How will you document parental interactions?
- How will students share their learning with their parents?
- How will you communicate with language-minority parents?
- How will you schedule for conferences?
- How will you gain parents' perspectives of student progress and instructional needs?
- How will you design your conference time?
- How will you determine whether or not you will incorporate the student in the conference?
- How will you decide what information you will share with parents?

Collegial Relationships

> " The plain truth is that the more we can work as a team and as teammates, the more probable our individual and joint success. "
>
> —THE MASTER TEACHER

School Community

Building positive relationships among your colleagues is critical to your overall job satisfaction and to maximizing the effectiveness of your school community.

The relationships you develop with administrators, mentors, grade level or department colleagues, and committee team members will help frame your professional practice. The resources available through these individuals will also lighten your load.

It is important to note the importance of reciprocation in these relationships. This includes your willingness to contribute to the professional tasks that influence the school community and to be open to feedback and input from your valued colleagues.

SUPPORT FROM AND ACCOUNTABILITY TO ADMINISTRATION

One of the goals of school and district administration is for all teachers to embrace the school community. Develop a respectful working relationship with your administration. Being competent and accountable in your professional role enhances your ability to solicit assistance when needed. Your administrator will support you in a variety of ways, for example, by setting up a mentoring relationship or directing you to systems of support.

MENTORING RELATIONSHIP

A mentoring relationship is one of the most valuable collegial relationships. Whether or not you are assigned a mentor or mentee, take initiative to engage in this impactful partnership by seeking a mentor or mentee, even in a more informal way.

Qualifications of an Effective Mentor

- Master classroom teacher
- Interpersonal skills
- Advocate for support of mentee
- Facilitator skills

Recommendations for Mentor/Mentee Match

- Consider grade and subject level
- Consider the physical proximity of mentor and mentee
- Consider both teachers' schedules

Log your interactions, and reflect for professional growth and development.

© 2008 Jupiter Images Corporation.

INTERACTIONS CONTACT LOG

Date	Beginning Time	Ending Time	Total Time	Contact Initiated by Beginning Teacher or Mentor Teacher	Type of Contact One-on-One/Phone Call/E-mail/Journal/ Drop-in Visit/Classroom Observation/ Conference/Other

EXPECTATIONS BEYOND THE CLASSROOM

In order for a school community to accomplish all that needs to be done, such as school improvement and extracurricular activities, educators must be involved in tasks beyond the classroom. Keep a running record of your collaborations, activities, and the follow-up needed, to ensure your committed professional responsibilities.

It is an expectation of teachers that they dedicate time to collaborate for achievement and create the various events that make their school an inviting, positive, inclusive place to learn. Decide your area of expertise, and participate in the writing committee, or help organize a school function. Not only do students benefit from these activities, but you will discover that you will too!

Grade Level or Department Teams Your grade level or department team will come to be a close group of colleagues. These are the people you will work with on a regular basis. Be sure to reciprocate the support they provide by contributing to the work effort of the group.

Sample Grade Level/Department Team Involvement

Leadership Opportunities within Grade Level/Department Teams

- Grade Level or Department Chair
- Textbook and Resource Materials Manager
- Curriculum Articulation Member
- School Improvement Team Liaison
- Classroom Management Articulation Representative
- Student Assessment Articulation Representative
- Inventory Manager
- Social Facilitator

Committees Your school and district will organize several committees in which you can participate. Choose one that aligns with your interests and schedule.

Sample Committee Involvement

Academic-Related Committees	Community-Building Committees
- School Improvement	- Back-to-School
- School Policies and Procedures	- Fall Festival
- Grade Level Specific Focus Groups	- Health and Wellness
- Student Standards Alignment	- Parent Advisory Board
- Curriculum Adoption	- Community Engagement

PROFESSIONAL COMMUNICATIONS LOG

Date_____

Contact initiated by: _____ Position/Role: _____

Person contacted: _____ Position/Role: _____

Purpose: _____

_____

_____

_____

Follow-Up

Date_____

Contact initiated by: _____ Position/Role: _____

Person contacted: _____ Position/Role: _____

Purpose: _____

_____

_____

_____

Follow-Up

Date_____

Contact initiated by: _____ Position/Role: _____

Person contacted: _____ Position/Role: _____

Purpose: _____

_____

_____

_____

Follow-Up

■ © Paulaphoto 2008. Used under license from Shutterstock, Inc.

Sponsorships Many extracurricular activities for students require a teacher sponsor. This type of commitment, although requiring concentrated time, allows you to build your relationships with students and get to know them better. Consider your strengths and interests when choosing an activity to sponsor.

Sample Sponsorship Involvement

Academic-Related Sponsorships	Activity-Related Sponsorships
■ Ecology	■ Athletics
■ Chess Club	■ Fine Arts
■ Technology	■ Student Council
■ Literary Publications	■ Peer Mediation
■ Academic Decathlon	■ Extra Mile Service

Support Personnel

SCHOOL OR DISTRICT PERSONNEL

There are several professionals who are considered support personnel who will also assist your efforts. Not every school or school district will employ all the personnel listed. However, some assistance will be available within any given school or district. Support personnel include:

- Special education teachers
- Reading and Title I teachers
- School psychologists
- Counselors
- School staff
- Social workers
- Nurses
- ESL/ELL teachers
- Speech or language specialists
- Physical and occupational therapists
- Vocational teachers and coordinators
- Specialists for the hearing or visually impaired
- Media specialists

EDUCATIONAL SUPPORT TEAMS

Educational support teams have been implemented in many school systems to help you solve instructional and social/behavior problems. Using a number of different names, including "building assistance team" or "school-wide assistance team," the team typically consists of multiple educators, elected by their peers, who provide assistance to teachers in meeting the needs of all students in their classrooms. Check for district-level and school-identified support teams in your education community.

best PRACTICES

Briscoe and Peters conclude that collaboration among teachers plays an important role in assisting teachers to reflect on their teaching. The results of the study indicate that collaboration facilitates change because it provides opportunities for teachers to learn both content and pedagogical knowledge from one another, encourages teachers to be risk takers in implementing new ideas, and supports and sustains the processes of individual change in science teaching.

Briscoe, C., & Peters, J. (1997). Teacher collaboration across and within schools: Supporting individual change in elementary science writing. *Science Education, 81,* 51–65.

Questions for Reflection

evaluation QUESTIONS

- In what ways will you establish and maintain collegial collaborations?

- How will you design a system of support to accommodate the diverse needs of your students?

COLLEGIAL RELATIONSHIPS

- How will you get to know key personnel?
- How will you obtain curriculum resources from the librarian or media specialist?
- How will you co-plan curriculum with grade level or department members?
- How will you build your relationship with your mentor?
- How will you communicate classroom successes with your administrator?
- How will you decide which classroom challenges to take to your administrator?

SUPPORT PERSONNEL

- How will you learn district-level resources?
- How will you become familiar with school-level support resources?

Self-Assessment of Professional Growth

Name			Date		
Grade Level/Content Area					

Parent Interactions	Low				High
To what degree do I have the knowledge needed for designing my classroom Back-to-School Night and Open House?	1 ☐	2 ☐	3 ☐	4 ☐	5 ☐
To what degree do I have the skills needed for designing my classroom Back-to-School Night and Open House?	1 ☐	2 ☐	3 ☐	4 ☐	5 ☐
Ongoing Parental Contacts	Low				High
To what degree do I have the knowledge needed for sustaining ongoing communication with parents?	1 ☐	2 ☐	3 ☐	4 ☐	5 ☐
To what degree do I have the skills needed for sustaining ongoing communication with parents?	1 ☐	2 ☐	3 ☐	4 ☐	5 ☐
Collegial Relationships	Low				High
To what degree do I have the knowledge needed to establish and maintain collegial collaborations?	1 ☐	2 ☐	3 ☐	4 ☐	5 ☐
To what degree do I have the skills needed to establish and maintain collegial collaborations?	1 ☐	2 ☐	3 ☐	4 ☐	5 ☐
Support Personnel	Low				High
To what degree do I have the knowledge needed to design a system of support to accommodate the diverse needs of my students?	1 ☐	2 ☐	3 ☐	4 ☐	5 ☐
To what degree do I have the skills needed to design a system of support to accommodate the diverse needs of my students?	1 ☐	2 ☐	3 ☐	4 ☐	5 ☐

Next Steps

Set goals for next steps to implement best practices in the teaching standard area of collaboration.

_____

_____

_____

_____

_____

_____

_____

_____

_____

_____

_____

_____

_____

_____

_____

_____

_____

_____

_____

Professional Development: Managing Reflective Growth

6

> **"** Seeing yourself as you want to be is the key to personal growth. **"**
>
> —UNKNOWN

Becoming a skilled and effective professional takes times and dedication. It also takes the process of experience. Make the most of the opportunities available to you within your district for enhancing your knowledge and skills as a teacher. Also, consider a more formal advancement through a degree program at a university. Remember, many states require professional development to maintain certification. The combination of meeting these requirements with the desire to be a life-long learner will help you evolve as a quality educator.

POINTS OF INQUIRY

- What strategies will you implement to manage yourself in your professional role?
- How will you provide meaningful closure to year-end for your students?
- What will your action plan include for closing down the school year?
- How will you resource your professional development to capitalize on your strengths and improve in areas needed for refinement?

Teacher Self-Management

> ❝The strongest principle of growth lies in human choice.❞
>
> —GEORGE ELLIOT

Know Yourself

Research has shown that teachers enter the field with anticipation of their career and the impact they will have on students. The complexity of teaching soon becomes a reality. The workload increases and the demands are endless. Physical well-being is a concern. Teachers must be intentional about managing themselves professionally, to balance their responsibilities for teacher and student success.

THE ARRAY INTERACTION MODEL

The first step in self-management is self-knowledge. Knowing yourself, your strengths, values, responses to stress, and sources of energy will enable you to function at your optimum and enjoy your life's work. The Array Interaction Model (Knaupp, 1995) and Array Management Model (Kortman, 1997) provides a tool for revealing who you are, for analysis and action. Four personality components are identified called "Personal Objectives." Every person has all four components within their personality composition; however, one component tends to dominate the way a person perceives/responds to life. The following graph describes how each personality component/personal objective responds in both a positive (cooperative) state and a stress (reluctant) state. You may recognize qualities of your own personality for both your primary and secondary personal objectives. Refer back to the Array Interaction Inventory completed in Chapter 2.

Personal Objective/Personality Components

	Harmony	Production	Connection	Status Quo
Cooperative (Positive State)	• Caring • Sensitive • Nurturing • Harmonizing • Feeling-oriented	• Logical • Structured • Organized • Systematic • Thinking-oriented	• Spontaneous • Creativity • Playful • Enthusiastic • Action-oriented	• Quiet • Imaginative • Insightful • Reflective • Inaction-oriented
Reluctant (Stress Responses)	• Over adaptive • Overpleasing • Makes mistakes • Cries • Giggles • Self-defeating • Depressed	• Overcritical • Overworks • Perfectionist • Verbally attacks • Demanding • Complaining • Take charge	• Disruptive • Blames • Irresponsible • Demands attention • Defiant • Breaking rules • Physically aggressive	• Disengaging • Withdrawn • Delays • Despondent • Daydreams • Indecisive • Silent treatment

Depending on your personality, you have a tendency to be stressed by specific things and respond to stressors in different ways. Stress can be defined as any stimulus that interferes with normal equilibrium and can produce physical, mental, or emotional tension. Stress can be a positive motivational force, but too much stress can become disruptive to a person's life and health.

Mentor Voices

➤ "Design active, hands-on projects toward the end of the year. This allows students to expend their energy while learning."

TEACHER SCENARIOS

The following teacher profiles highlight some predictable responses from teachers in both positive and stressful moments. Which ones do you identify with?

Harmony Jennifer's response on the "Array Interaction Survey" indicates she rates high in the Harmony Personal Objective. When in a normal state (cooperative), she is caring and pro-social. Her relationships with her students, and with family and friends, are important to her. She enjoys the school community and feels privileged to be impacting the lives of her students.

When highly stressed, Jennifer tends to over adapt, overplease and make mistakes on the most routine items. Jennifer tends to be stressed by large amounts of paperwork, lack of social time with colleagues, and not enough time to have one-on-one interactions with students. She may procrastinate, waste time by socializing, and then feel badly because she doesn't have time for family, friends, or tasks that must be completed. She has a poor filing system, which intensifies her paper dilemma. She also has a difficult time saying "no" and frequently finds herself on "one too many" committees and planning teams with a schedule that is overwhelming.

Production Mia's survey indicates she has a Production Personal Objective. She is logical, structured, organized, and persistent. She is a thinker, a problem-solver, likes information exchange, and values such things as using time efficiently, task completion, skill development and schedules. Mia has many ideas and enjoys sharing them with colleagues. She is efficient, and her desk, lesson plans, and materials are always well organized She is most likely to become stressed by changes in scheduling, too many unnecessary meetings, and confusing job descriptions, interruptions, or lack of specific information.

When Mia is stressed, she may become critical of herself and others. She may verbally disagree with a colleague's actions. She may put undue pressure on herself to do things perfectly, even neglecting to eat in order to finish a task. She tends to become curt when colleagues "waste her time" by engaging in frivolous chatter when she knows she could be accomplishing other more relevant tasks with her valuable time.

Connection Billie rated herself as having a Connection Personal Objective. She loves activity and action and enters a room with energy. She is friendly, connects with others in positive ways, enjoys music and drama, and is very creative. She likes to try new things, and never teaches the same material the same way twice. She enjoys the spontaneous moment.

When stressed, Billie can become irresponsible, disruptive, attention-getting, and blaming. Her jokes may become inappropriate and sarcastic. She can become openly defiant. Billie is stressed by high levels of structure when there is no room for creative thought or spontaneity.

Status Quo Jose's survey results identify Status Quo as his Personal Objective. Jose is very quiet and reserved, insightful and reflective. When he speaks, both colleagues and students listen. He is good at repetitive tasks, and enjoys putting lessons together on the computer, and finding out additional information and activities from resources on the Internet.

When Jose becomes stressed, he begins to withdraw. He may lack enthusiasm, and demonstrates little effort. He allows the students to do their own thing and does not pull it all back together for closure. He may sit at his desk to grade papers and find that 20 minutes has elapsed. Jose is most likely to be stressed by lack of specific direction and insufficient information. He is also stressed by too much activity with no break time for regrouping his thoughts and feelings.

Identifying and Modifying Stress

ENERGY DRAINS

Stress drains your energy, lowers your personal motivation, and frequently hinders your ability to solve problems and meet daily challenges. It is important to specify stressors so that you can avoid them, adjust to them, and redirect your behavior. Learning how to deal with your stressors and subsequent energy drains are essential. The following examples follow Jennifer, Mia, Billie and Jose as they learn to self-manage.

Harmony Jennifer is anxious about the large amount of paperwork associated with progress reports. As soon as school is dismissed for the day, Jennifer is going to generate a list of the things she needs to accomplish before the next school day, and prioritize the list. She is going to allow herself a 10-minute break to socialize and get a snack before returning to the classroom to implement the plan.

Production Mia is frustrated by not getting through her to-do list and accomplishing all that was included. Mia is going to allow 20 minutes in her schedule to adjust for any unplanned time demands. She will pack a nutritious snack for mid-morning recess so that her physical energy is rejuvenated even before mid-day.

Connection Billie is pressured by the curricular and testing demands for her grade level. Billie is going to plan a variety of learning tasks that both meet lesson objectives and engage herself and students actively in the learning process.

Status Quo Jose becomes indifferent when multiple activities are vying for his attention. Jose will stay in his room during lunch to give himself a chance to regroup and deliberately plan for any adjustments needed for the rest of the day.

PROACTIVE PLANNING

Identify constructive ways to manage your stress. Begin by thinking about activities or responsibilities that lead to energy drains and initiate stress responses. Consider specific actions to reduce the "energy drains." The following sections will provide the next steps in your proactive plan, which include identifying your needs and building on the things that generate positive energy.

Energy Drains List what drains your energy.	Proactive Plan Identify actions to reduce or eliminate energy drains.

IDENTIFYING NEEDS

In the last sections you considered:

- your primary and secondary personality components (Personal Objectives);
- what activities/responsibilities stress you;
- how you personally respond to stress;
- ways to proactively manage your stress.

When you consider your personality, it is important to understand what you need in order to stay in a positive and cooperative mode of interaction. It is important to know yourself and proactively plan ways to accommodate for your own psychological needs.

Jennifer, Mia, Billie, and Jose identify specific ways their personality needs are met within the classroom context.

Harmony Jennifer values collegial relationships and positive student relationships, and needs a comforting work environment that is aesthetically pleasing to her.

Production Mia values accomplishment and needs to feel appreciated for her work efforts. Mia also needs an organized work environment.

Connection Billie values activity and needs to experience positive engagement and participation in her work environment. She needs to be involved in stimulating activity.

Status Quo Jose values privacy and stability. He needs quiet time in the day to think and prepare. Jose also needs predictable routines and schedules.

The following chart shows the primary needs associated with each personality and some possible ideas for ways to meet those needs.

Needs Chart

	Harmony	Production	Connection	Status Quo
Psychological needs	• Values self/others • Sensory experiences	• Value for work • Time schedule	• Values action • Fun activity	• Values time • Stability
Ways to meet need	• Value feelings • Comfortable surroundings • Personal effects (family photos, etc.) • Time with colleagues	• Value ideas • Incentives • To-do list • Routine for the day • Organization	• Value activity • Hands-on activities • Group interaction • Change in routine	• Value quietness • Independent activities • Computer activities • Routine tasks

My Needs Identify primary psychological needs.	**Proactive Plan** Identify actions to meet needs.

BUILDING ENERGY GAINS

When your psychological needs are met, you feel confident, stronger, and more capable; in other words, you actually gain energy.

Think about actions or activities that energize you. Think of ways you can build these "Energy Gains" into your life.

Let's refer to our four example teachers:

- Jennifer socializes with colleagues for a few minutes after school.
- Following a to-do list makes Mia feel accomplished and in control of her time.
- Billie plays music while planning for the next day.
- Jose takes a few minutes to reflect in the quiet of his classroom.

Energy Gains List what energizes you.	Proactive Plan Identify actions to meet needs.

Warning Signs

Teaching is rewarding, challenging, and fulfilling, but at the same time it is demanding, energy-draining, and time-consuming. Too much stress can cause physical problems. Symptoms frequently associated with severe stress include:

- Recurring headaches
- Laryngitis
- Stomach problems
- Frequent heartburn
- Hostile feelings/language
- Depression/crying
- Sudden weight changes
- Tense back/neck muscles
- Unrelenting exhaustion

If you are experiencing any of these symptoms, or a combination of these symptoms, it is important that you seek a doctor's attention. Mental and physical stress symptoms are your body's way of telling you to reflect and put balance into your life. Remember, a well-balanced teacher can productively embrace each new day.

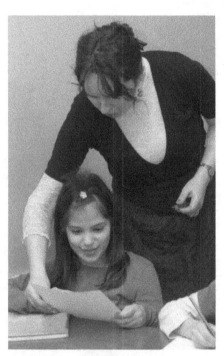
© PhotoCreate 2008. Used under license from Shutterstock, Inc.

Stress Relievers

Use the following stress relievers to gain positive energy.

- Stand up and do stretching exercises.
- Close your eyes and think of a color; picture five objects of that color.
- Close your eyes and visualize your greatest achievement.
- Crumple up a piece of paper and play "basketball" using your trashcan.
- Drink a glass of water with small sips.
- List five things you have enjoyed in the last month.
- List five things you would like to do in the next month.
- Think of some funny event from your life. Laugh out loud.
- Color a picture in a coloring book.
- Take three deep, slow breaths in and out.

best PRACTICES

One of the characteristics of teaching is the complexity of the work. At times it can be overwhelming. Teachers report in studies done by Kortman and Honaker (2005) that acknowledgement of stress and becoming aware of how to manage, allows teachers to balance their work and personal lives. Also, by being conscious of stressors, teachers can sense and seek support during their working day to remain in cooperative behavior. Teachers will have greater gains in their effectiveness in the classroom.

Kortman, S., & Honaker, C. (2005). *The BEST beginning teacher experience: A framework for professional development with CD-ROM.* Dubuque, IA: Kendall/Hunt Publishing Company.

Questions for Reflection

evaluation QUESTIONS ?

- What strategies will you implement to manage yourself in your professional role?
- How will you provide meaningful closure to year-end for your students?

SELF-MANAGEMENT

- How will you determine your primary and secondary personality/ Personal Objectives?
- How will you identify stressors?
- How will you plan to respond appropriately to stress?
- How will you take care of yourself to stay positive?
- How will you create a comfortable work environment?

CLOSURE WITH STUDENTS

- How will you decide special learning projects for closing down the year?
- How will you include meaningful reflection for your students?
- How will you leave a legacy for what you want your students to think, know, and believe after their year with you?
- How will you celebrate each student in your classroom?
- How will you have your students say goodbye to you and their friends?
- How will you say "thank you" to your students' parents?

A Purposeful Closure

> **"**He who has put a good finish to his undertaking
> is said to have placed a golden crown to the whole.**"**
>
> —EUSTATHIUS

Until the Last Bell Rings

At this time of year many students sense "the end is near" and often act accordingly. There is often a misperception that the end of the school year is not academically meaningful but only filled with "time-consuming" activities. However, you want to convey the message that the end of the school year is filled with rich opportunities for learning. This is also a time to engage the students in ways that they will:

- acknowledge the classroom community
- celebrate their own personal abilities and talents
- consider ways they can learn throughout the summer
- look forward to coming back to school next year.

SPECIAL LEARNING PROJECTS

In most states, standardized testing is completed in April. In many cases the required curriculum has been taught prior to state testing. Therefore, many expert teachers use this time to deliver high-interest instructional projects that offer opportunities for children to apply the skills they have learned. They also incorporate remedial units for student mastery of content.

STUDENT REFLECTIONS

Students need time to reflect upon the learning experiences they shared with you and their classmates. The following activities focus on summarizing the learning that students experienced and will hopefully store in their memories.

Personal Scrapbook Have each student create a personal scrapbook of their year. The students can include such items as:

- summary of the content learned
- work from their portfolio
- snapshots of them engaged in classroom activities
- other meaningful artifacts related to the class.

They may take this treasure home on the last day of school.

Top Ten List Have each student make a top ten list of their favorite memories, themes, projects, units of instruction, and videos from the year. They may personalize it in their own unique way.

view POINT

Try to keep classroom schedules and activities as routine as possible until year end.

Closure with Students

You have spent the better part of a year with the students in your classroom. They have made an emotional impact on you and you have probably touched their lives in more ways than you'll ever know. Just as you planned their academic lessons every day, it is now equally important for you to consider how you will plan to send them to the next grade level. Beyond their academic skills, you need to consider how you want them to feel about themselves as students and people. Saying goodbye to your students means you will need to consider:

> **viewPOINT**
>
> Reflection exercises not only help the students recall their learning experiences, but they also allow the teacher to see what instructional activities students value most.

- what memories you want them to have of their year with you
- what learning legacies of themselves you want them to form
- what meaningful ways they can close out the year with each other.

Making Memories Take a few moments and list three things you would like your students to think, believe, or know after their year with you. These will become their memories of you and their learning legacy. Plan some specific ways you will embrace these into your end-of-year planning.

What I want my students to think, believe, and know:	Specific ways I will integrate this into my planning:

Individual Conferences Take 3–5 minutes to share something very personalized and sincere with each student. Your comments may include your perceptions of their contributions to the classroom, identification of an individual trait or ability you admire, or encouragement of continuous growth in their strengths.

Personal Note Compose a letter or note to each student in your classroom. Describe your appreciation of the talents, qualities, or contributions they have made to you, other students, or the classroom during the year.

Special Certificates Create an individualized "certificate" for each student. Each certificate is unique, and highlights the students' special talents, qualities, characteristics or abilities. The goal is for each student to feel pride in the area identified. Be sure to think of how each student's parent will interpret the area of recognition. Remember, being awarded the "Most Improved" may be interpreted as a negative, not a positive. Positive examples include:

Academic Excellence	Independent	Dedicated
Risk-Taker	Cooperative	Loyal
Artistic	Helpful	Committed
Inquisitive	Musical	Critical Thinker
Diligent	Athletic	Problem Solver
Persistent	Optimistic	Courteous
Respectful	Awesome Attitude	Generous
Compassionate	Positive Thinker	Polite
Friendly	Honest	Gracious
Personable	Caring	
Confident	Active Listener	

view POINT

The students will want to say thank you and goodbye to classroom aides, parent helpers, and school personnel. Design cards for students to sign and deliver.

Classroom Message Board Have a large poster or banner of butcher paper for the students to share written compliments to one another. Be sure everyone has something positive written about them by the end of the day.

CLOSURE WITH PARENTS

Summary Letter Your students have learned so much during the school year. Many parents appreciate a summary letter to review the major academic units and learning achievements. To begin this summary, it is helpful to review your long-term plans. You might wish to highlight academic units and special events from the students' perspectives.

Satisfaction Survey Toward the end of the spring semester, many schools routinely ask parents to complete a survey about their satisfaction with the curriculum, the school, and the teacher. Often the teacher is asked to send the survey home with the students and then collect the information for the school administration to summarize. In some schools the survey is sent directly to the parents via the mail or accomplished through an online format. However the data is collected, it is important for the parents to have an opportunity to give feedback to the teacher and the school. If your school does not collect this type of information, you may wish to develop a questionnaire.

Recognition Tea The parents, like the students, have played an important part in your classroom community. Therefore, it is important to recognize their contributions. Many principals sponsor a school-wide, end-of-the-year celebration for parents who have volunteered in various ways throughout the year.

If the school does not sponsor the celebration, it is a good idea to invite the parents to attend the end-of-the-year party. The students can help make special recognition cards. A heartfelt thank you is always appreciated.

Summer Activities Teachers may wish to send home a Summer Activity Packet on the last day of school. The packet may include:

- age-appropriate learning;
- a listing of local programs that are sponsored by the city or local university;
- a reminder of summer safety tips.

Until the Key Is Turned In

In many ways the end of the school year is as challenging as the start. There are dozens of details and administrative requirements that must be completed. Plan ahead to accomplish the tasks while enjoying this important season of the school year.

CLOSURE WITH COLLEAGUES

Though you will see most of your colleagues and administrators next year, it is a wise idea to compose thank you notes or emails for people who have helped you throughout the year. These could include the principal, assistant principal, nurse, secretary, custodian and your grade-level teammates. While it takes a few minutes to write your appreciation, the recipients of your thanks will greatly appreciate them.

CLOSING DOWN YOUR CLASSROOM

Do you remember the hours you spent at the beginning of the year setting up your classroom? Well, the good news is that it will take less time to take it down than it did to put it up. The bad news is that you have accumulated a lot and will probably have much more to put away.

Organizational Scheme As you put away teaching materials you will also need to consider how to organize your instructional units so that you may retrieve them easily next year. Some teachers use a subject-by-subject approach, while others use a month-by-month scheme. Teachers who use an integrated approach will store materials by thematic units.

© 2008 Jupiter Images Corporation.

Check-Out List In addition to organizing your teaching materials, you will need to accomplish a number of administrative tasks. Most schools provide a list of actions you must complete before the end of the school year. The following list provides examples of end-of-year responsibilities:

- ❑ Submit gradebooks with class rosters and attendance sheets.
- ❑ Insert grades onto a permanent file card for each individual student.
- ❑ Return all software and A. V. materials to the learning resource or media center.
- ❑ Return curriculum materials or teacher editions.
- ❑ Return textbooks, manipulatives, and learning aids to designated storage areas.
- ❑ Return all school-owned equipment/materials to designated areas for storage.
- ❑ Turn in textbook lists and requested-purchase orders for next year.
- ❑ Turn in completed list of schedule preferences for next year's class schedule.
- ❑ Turn in recommendations for next year's student placements.
- ❑ Submit completed supply requests and standard stock requisitions.
- ❑ Clear classroom walls.
- ❑ Return next year's teacher contract to Human Resources.
- ❑ Provide district/school office with summer addresses and telephone numbers.
- ❑ Return all keys.
- ❑ Pick up paycheck from building administrator when entire list is complete.

Reflections: Identifying Professional and Personal Goals

The end of the school year is a perfect time to reflect upon the accomplishments of the past year. It is a time to consider:

- what you learned and what you still want to know
- what you did well and what you want to do better.

The guided-reflection form will help you to review your year, celebrate your triumphs, and establish new goals.

The outcome I am most pleased with from this year is . . .

The thing I am most disappointed about from this year is . . .

The part of teaching that is most natural for me is . . .

The part of teaching that is the most difficult for me is . . .

The one thing that I could not have been prepared for, regardless of preparation, is . . .

The best part of teaching is . . .

My professional goals include . . .

A purposeful closure for a teacher is really a new beginning.

best PRACTICES

"Becoming a reflective, research-oriented educator paves the way for meeting the challenge of today's evolving, diverse, standards-centered classroom, as well as for taking charge of one's own professional growth" (Parsons, 2004). Teachers need to become reflective practitioners and engage in their teaching through a research mind set. This will encourage teachers to view instructional, environmental, or behavioral changes as interventions that can lead to efficient and effective classroom learning."

Parsons, S. (2004, October). Reflective Research. In S. L. Bisenger (Ed.), *teachertoday . . .* , 20(2), 3–4.

evaluation QUESTIONS

- What will your action plan include for closing down the school year?

- How will you resource your professional development to capitalize on your strengths and improve in areas needed for refinement?

Questions for Reflection

CLOSING DOWN THE SCHOOL YEAR

- How will you close down your classroom?
- How will you thank those who have assisted you this school year?

PROFESSIONAL DEVELOPMENT

- How will you reflect on your year and your accomplishments?
- How will you implement professional development goals into your summer and your next school year?

Reflection: Self-Assessment of Professional Growth

Name				Date	
Grade Level/Content Area					
Self-Management	Low				High
To what degree do I have the knowledge needed to self-manage my professional role?	1 ☐	2 ☐	3 ☐	4 ☐	5 ☐
To what degree do I have the skills needed to self-manage my professional role?	1 ☐	2 ☐	3 ☐	4 ☐	5 ☐
Closure with Students	Low				High
To what degree do I have the knowledge needed to provide a meaningful closure to year-end for my students?	1 ☐	2 ☐	3 ☐	4 ☐	5 ☐
To what degree do I have the teaching skills needed to provide a meaningful closure to year-end for my students?	1 ☐	2 ☐	3 ☐	4 ☐	5 ☐
Closing Down the School Year	Low				High
To what degree do I have the knowledge needed to develop an action plan for closing down the school year?	1 ☐	2 ☐	3 ☐	4 ☐	5 ☐
To what degree do I have the teaching skills needed to develop an action plan for closing down the school year?	1 ☐	2 ☐	3 ☐	4 ☐	5 ☐
Professional Development	Low				High
To what degree do I have the knowledge needed to resource my professional development to capitalize on my strengths and improve in areas needed for refinement?	1 ☐	2 ☐	3 ☐	4 ☐	5 ☐
To what degree do I have the teaching skills needed to resource my professional development to capitalize on my strengths and improve in areas needed for refinement?	1 ☐	2 ☐	3 ☐	4 ☐	5 ☐

Next Steps

Set goals for next steps to implement best practices in the teaching standard of professional development.

_____

_____

_____

_____

_____

_____

_____

_____

_____

_____

_____

_____

_____

_____

_____

_____

_____

_____

_____

_____

_____

REFERENCES

Algozzine, B., Ysseldyke, J., & Elliot, J. (1997). *Strategies and tactics for effective instruction.* Longmont, CO: Sopris West.

Apacki, C. (1991). *Energize! Energizers and other great cooperative activities for all ages.* Granville, OH: Quest Books.

Arends, R.I. (2003). *Learning to teach.* New York, NY: McGraw-Hill, Inc.

Barootchi, N., & Keshavarz, M. (2002). Assessment of achievement through portfolios and teacher-made tests. *Educational Research, 44*(3), 279–288.

Becker, H., & Epstein, J. (1982). Parent involvement: A study of teacher practices. *Elementary School Journal, 83*(2), 85–102.

Black, P., & William, D. (1998). Inside the black box: Raising standards through classroom assessment. *Phi Delta Kappan, 80*(2), 139–148.

Bloom, B.S., et al. (Eds.). (1984). *Taxonomy of educational objectives book 1: Cognitive domain.* White Plains, NY: Longman Publishing.

Bradley, D.F., King-Sears, M.E., & Tessierr-Switlick, D.M. (1997). *Teaching students in inclusive settings: From theory to practice.* Boston, MA: Allyn & Bacon.

Briscoe, C., & Peters, J. (1997). Teacher collaboration across and within schools: Supporting individual change in elementary science writing. *Science Education, 81*(1), 51–65.

Brooke, D.M., & Hawke, G. (1985). *Effective and ineffective session opening: Teacher activity and task structures.* Paper presented at the American Educational Research Association, Chicago, IL.

Bybee, R.W., et al. (2006). *The BSCS 5e instructional model: Origins, effectiveness, and applications.* Colorado Springs, CO: Office of Science Education, National Institute of Health.

Canter, L., & Canter, M. (2001). *Assertive discipline: Positive behavior management for today's classroom* (3rd ed.). Los Angeles, CA: Canter and Associates.

Carlson, A.C. (1991). *Family questions.* New Brunswick, NJ: Transaction.

Cawthorne, B. (1987). *Instant success for classroom teachers new and substitute teachers.* Scottsdale, AZ: Greenfield Publications.

Charles, C.M. (2008). *Building classroom discipline* (8th ed.). White Plains, NY: Longman Publishing.

Christie, J., Enz, B., & Vukelich, C. (2002). *Teaching language and literacy: Preschool through the elementary grades* (2nd ed.). New York, NY: Addison, Wesley, Longman Publishing.

Collier, V. (1989). How long: A synthesis of research on academic achievement in a second language. *TESOL Quarterly, 23*, 509–531.

Collins, Cathy. (1987). *Time management for teachers: Practical techniques and skills that give you more time to teach.* Mira Loma, CA: Parker Publishing.

Cruickshank, D.R., Bainer, D., & Metcalf, K. (2005). *The act of teaching.* New York, NY: McGraw-Hill.

Cummins, J. (1981). The role of primary language development in promoting educational success for language minority students. In C. Leyba, *Schooling and Language Minority Students: A Theoretical Framework.* Los Angeles, CA: California State University, Evaluation, Dissemination and Assessment Center.

Dreikurs, R., Cassel, P., & Ferguson, E. (2004). *Discipline without tears: How to reduce conflict and establish cooperation in the classroom.* Mississauga, Ontario: John Wiley and Sons.

Drummond, K. V., & Stipek, D. (2004, January). Low income parents' beliefs about their role in children's academic learning. *The Elementary School Journal, 104*(3), 197–213.

Dyck, N., Pemberton, J., Woods, K., & Sundbye, N. (1996). *Creating inclusive schools: A new design for all students.* Lawrence, KS: Curriculum Solutions, Inc.

Edwards, C.H. (2007). *Classroom discipline and management.* Mississauga, Ontario: John Wiley and Sons.

Emmer, E.T., & Evertson, C. (1980). *Effective management at the beginning of the school year in junior high classes.* Austin, TX: Research and Development Center for Teacher Education, The University of Texas, Austin.

Emmer, E.T., & Evertson, C. (1981, January). Synthesis of research on classroom management. *Educational Leadership, 38*(4), 342–347.

Emmer, E.T., et al. (2002). *Classroom management for secondary teachers* (6th ed.). Boston, MA: Allyn & Bacon.

Enk, J., & Hendricks, M. (1981). *Shortcuts for teachers: Strategies for reducing classroom workload.* Belmont, CA: Pitman Learning, Inc.

Enz, B., & Kimerer, K. (2000). *Teachers—How To Win the Job You Want.* Dubuque, IA: Kendall/Hunt Publishing.

Enz, B., Hurwitz, S, & Carlile, B. (2005). T*he student teacher experience: A developmental approach* (3rd ed.). Dubuque, IA: Kendall/Hunt Publishing.

Enz, B. J., Bergeron, B., & Wolfe, M. (2006). *Learning to teach.* Dubuque, IA: Kendall/Hunt Publishing.

Epstein, J. (1986). Parent's reactions to teacher practices of parent involvement. *Elementary School Journal, 86*(3), 277–294.

Evertson, C.M., Emmer, E.T., Clements, B.S., Sanford, J.P., & Worsham, M.E. (2005). *Classroom management for elementary teachers.* Boston, MA: Allyn & Bacon.

Field, M.V., Spangler, K.L., & Lee, D.M. (2007). *Let's begin reading right: Developmentally appropriate beginning literacy.* Upper Saddle River, NJ: Prentice Hall.

Flaxman, E., & Inger, M. (1991). Parents and schooling in the 1990s. *Principal, 72*(2), 16–18.

Fredericks, A.D., & Rasinski, T.V. (1990). Involving the uninvolved: How to. *The Reading Teacher, 43*, 424–425.

Gelfer, J.I. (1991). Teacher-parent partnerships: Enhancing communications. *Childhood Education, 67*, 164–167.

Giangreco, M.R., Colinger, C.J., & Iverson, V.S. (1993). *Choosing options and accommodations for children.* Baltimore, MD: Paul Brookes.

Glasser, W. (2000). *Every student can succeed.* Chatsworth, CA: William Glasser.

Gordon, T. (2003). *Teacher effectiveness training: The program proven to help teachers bring out the best in students of all ages.* New York, NY: Three Rivers Press.

Hammeken, P.A. (2000). *450 strategies for success: A practical guide for all educators who teach students with disabilities.* Minnetonka, MN: Peytral Publications.

Harrison, A., & Burton Spuler, F. (1983*). Hot tips for teachers: A collection of classroom management ideas.* Belmont, CA: David S. Lake Publishers.

Hines, R.A., & Johnston, J.H. (1996). *Inclusive classrooms: The principal's role in promoting achievement.* Reston, VA: National Association of Secondary School Principals.

Individuals with Disabilities Education Act of 2004, 20 U.S.C. § 1400 (2004).

Jones, F. (2007). *Fred Jones tools for teaching: Discipline, instruction, motivation.* Santa Cruz, CA: Fredric H. Jones & Associates.

Jones, V.F., & Jones, L.S. (2006). *Comprehensive classroom management: Creating positive learning environments for all students* (8th ed.). Needham Heights, MA: Allyn & Bacon.

Kinchin, I. (2004). Investigating students' beliefs about their preferred role as learners. *Educational Research, 46*(3), 301–312.

Knaupp, J. (1995). *Array model.* Unpublished document. College of Education, Arizona State University, Tempe, AZ.

Kortman, S. (1997). *I know me: Personal objective response sheet.* College of Education, Arizona State University, Tempe, AZ.

Kortman, S.A., & Honaker, C.J. (2002). *The BEST beginning teacher experience: A framework for professional development.* Dubuque, IA: Kendall/Hunt Publishing.

Kortman, S.A., & Honaker, C.J. (2002). *The BEST mentoring experience: A framework for professional development.* Dubuque, IA: Kendall/Hunt Publishing.

Kortman, S.A., & Honaker, C.J. (2005). *The BEST standards in teaching: Reflection to quality practice.* Dubuque, IA: Kendall/Hunt Publishing.

Kounin, J. (1977). *Discipline and groups management in classrooms.* Huntington, NY: R.E. Krieger Publishing.

Kronowitz, E.L. (2003). *Your first year of teaching and beyond* (4th ed.). Upper Saddle River, NY: Prentice Hall.

Lipsky, D.K., & Gartner, A. (1997). *Inclusion and school reform*. Baltimore, MD: Paul H. Brookes Publishing.

Lovitt, T.C. (1997). *Special Education: Common questions, common-sense answers*. Longmont, CO: Sopris West.

Manera, E. (1996). *Substitute teaching: Planning for success*. West Lafayette, IN: Kappa Delta Pi Publications.

Marzano, R.J., Pickering, D.J., & Pollack, J.E. (2001). *Classroom instruction that works: Research-based strategies for increasing student achievement*. Alexandria, VA: Association of Curriculum Development.

McCoy, M.K. (1995). *Teaching special learners in the general education classroom*. Denver, CO: Love Publishing.

McLaughlin, B. (1992). Myths and misconceptions about second language learning: What every teacher needs to unlearn. *National Center for Research on Cultural Diversity and Second Language Learning*, 1–9.

Montgomery, J.K. (1996). Selected strategies for inclusive classrooms. In Florian L. and Rouse, M. (Eds.). *School Reform and Special Educational Needs: Anglo-American Perspectives*. Cambridge, MA: University of Cambridge Institute of Education.

Moore, E. (1991, September). Improving schools through parental involvement. *Principal, 71*(1), 17, 19–20.

Peregoy S., & Boyle, O. (2004). *Reading writing and learning in ESL: A resource book for K–12 teachers*. Upper Saddle River, NJ: Prentice Hall.

Pugach, M.C., & Warger, C. L. (Eds.). (1996). *Curriculum trends, special education, and reform: Refocusing the conversation*. New York. NY: Teachers College Press.

Putnam, J.K. (Ed.). (1998). *Cooperative learning and strategies for inclusion: Celebrating diversity in the classroom*. Baltimore, MD: Paul H. Brookes Publishing.

Quinton, D., & Rutter, M. (1988). *Parenting breakdown: The making and breaking of inter-generational links*. Aldershot, England: Avebury.

Rennie, J. (1993). *ESL and bilingual program models*. Washington, DC: ERIC Digest. (ERIC Document Reproduction Service No. ED362072).

Sanford, J.D., & Evertson, C.M. (1980). *Beginning the school year at a low SES junior high: Three case studies* (R&D Report No. 6104). Austin, TX: Research and Development Center for Teacher Education. (ERIC Document Reproduction Service No. ED195547).

Skinner, B.F. (1998). The experimental analysis of operant behavior: A history. In R.W. Rieber and K. Salzinger (Eds.), *Psychology: Theoretical-historical perspectives* (2nd ed.). New York, NY: American Psychological Association.

Skrtic, T.M. (Ed.) (1995). *Disability and democracy: Reconstructing (special) education for postmodernity*. New York, NY: Teachers College Press.

Slavin, R.E. (1995). *Cooperating learning* (2nd ed.). Needham Heights, MA: Allyn & Bacon.

Spandel, V. (2008). *Creating writers through 6-trait writing assessment and instruction*. Boston, MA: Allyn & Bacon.

St. Michel, T. (1994). *Substitute teachers: Who? What? How? When? Where? Why? A case study of the substitute process*. Unpublished doctoral dissertation, Arizona State University.

Stainback, S., & Stainback, W. (1996). *Curriculum considerations in inclusive classrooms*. Baltimore, MD: Paul H. Brookes Publishing.

Stainback, S., & Stainback, W. (1996). *Inclusion: A guide for educators*. Baltimore, MD: Paul H. Brookes Publishing.

Tauber, R.T. (2007). *Classroom management: Sound theory and effective practice* (4th ed.). Westport, CT: Praeger Paperback.

Turnbull, A.P., & Turnbull, H.R., III. (2000). *Families, professionals, and exceptionality: A special partnership* (4th ed.). Upper Saddle River, NJ: Merrill/Prentice Hall.

Udvari-Solner, A. (1992). *Curricular adaptations: Accommodating the instructional needs of diverse learners in the context of general education*. Topeka, KS: Kansas State Board of Education.

Understanding the stages of a child's reading development (Report No. RCS-FAST-BIB-3). (1988). Bloomington, IN: Office of Educational Research and Implementation. (ERIC Document Reproduction Service No. ED293094).

Vaughn, S., Bos, C.S., & Schumm, J.S. (1997). *Teaching mainstreamed, diverse, and at-risk students in the general education classroom.* Boston, MA: Allyn & Bacon.

Villa, R., & Thousand, J. (1997). *The inclusion puzzle: Putting the pieces together.* Paper presented at the annual convention of the Council for Exceptional Children, Salt Lake City, UT.

Warner, J., Bryan, C., & Warner, D. (2006). *The unauthorized teacher's survival guide.* St. Paul, MN: JIST Publishing.

Williamson, B. (1998). *A first year teacher's guidebook: An educational recipe book for success* (2nd ed.). Sacramento, CA: Dynamic Teaching Company.

Willis, S. (1994). Teaching language-minority students: Role of native-language instruction is debated. *ASCD Update, 36*(5), 1, 4–5.

Winebrenner, S. (2001). *Teaching gifted kids in the regular classroom.* Minneapolis, MN: Free Spirit Publishing, Inc.

Wolfgang, C.H. (2005). *Solving discipline problems: Methods and models for today's teachers* (6th ed.). New York, NY: John Wiley & Sons.

INDEX

R

S